UNIQUE EATS AND EATERIES

OF

PHILADELPHIA

Library of Congress Control Number: 2018945699
ISBN: 9781681061412

Front cover photo credits left to right: Saté Kampar by Maria Young; Suraya by Melissa Alam; Hershel's Deli by Michael Chaney of Blackwater Promotions; Zahav courtesy of CookNSolo Restaurants; Di Bruno Bros.; McGillin's Olde Ale House; Reading Terminal Market; Metropolitan Bakery.

Back cover photo credits left to right: Irene Levy Baker by Rachel Baker. Top row: Camac Tavern; Di Bruno Bros.; Cook by Yoni Nimrod. Left side: Fork by Chaucee Stillman; Gran Caffe L'Aquila; Cheu Noodle Bar by Danya Henninger, Imagic Digital, La Colombe courtesy of La Colombe. Right side: Vietnam by Brett Thomas Photography; Mac Mart; Hungry Pigeon by Neal Santos. Bottom: London Grill.

Title page photo credits: Top row from left to right: Hershel's Deli by Michael Chaney, Blackwater Promotions. Vetri Cucina courtesy of Vetri Family. Saté Kampar by Kerry McIntyre. Oyster House by Jason Varney. Fork by Chaucee Stillman. Vernick by Clay Williams. Vetri Cucina courtesy of Vetri Family. Farmer's Keep courtesy of Farmer's Keep. Barbuzzo by Jason Varney. Vietnam Café & Restaurant by Brett Thomas Photography. Capogiro Gelato Artisans by Lexy Pierce. Vedge by Michael Spain Smith.

Printed in the United States of America
18 19 20 21 22   5 4 3 2

UNIQUE EATS AND EATERIES

OF

PHILADELPHIA

IRENE LEVY BAKER

Photo by Rachel Baker

CONTENTS

Introduction.. ix

Ten Tips for Getting Reservations at Philadelphia's

    Top Restaurants xi

John & Kira's.. 2

Will BYOB.. 4

Dante & Luigi's Corona di Ferro 6

Gran Caffè L'Aquila 8

Frieda 10

McGillin's Olde Ale House 12

Greensgrow Farms 14

Tavern on Camac 16

Vedge 18

Palizzi Social Club... 22

Bassetts Ice Cream.. 24

Hop Sing Laundromat... 26

Ambra... 28

Mr. Martino's Trattoria 30

Vientiane Café... 32

Portabellos of Kennett Square.................................... 34

Pop's Homemade Italian Ice 36

Miss Rachel's Pantry 38

Vietnam Café & Restaurant.. 40

Magpie 42

Saté Kampar... 44

Hershel's East Side Deli... 46

Zahav.. 48

Rooster Soup Company & Federal Donuts 50

EAT Café & Rosa's Fresh Pizza 52

El Compadre 54

RIM Café... 56

Suraya 58

Di Bruno Bros. 60

COOK 62

Feliz Restaurants 64

Oyster House 66

Hungry Pigeon 68

Fork 70

Vernick Food & Drink 72

Fishtown 74

Metropolitan Bakery 76

Cheu Noodle Bar 78

Termini Bros. Bakery 80

Speakeasies 82

London Grill 84

Talula's Table 86

Warmdaddy's 88

Philadelphia's Chinatown 90

City Tavern 92

Pizza Brain & Museum 94

Crêperie Beau Monde 96

South Philadelphia 98

Nuts to You 100

Japanese Tea Ceremony 102

Moshulu 104

The Franklin Fountain 106

Shane Confectionery 108

Culinary Literacy Center 110

Kaplan's New Model Bakery 112

Maison 208 114

Capogiro Gelato Artisans 134

Farmer's Keep and Sweet Freedom 136

Victor Cafe 140

La Colombe 142

Pretzels 144

Vetri Cucina 146

Reading Terminal Market 148

Chef's Counters 150

Ralph's Italian Restaurant 152

Philadelphia's Craft Breweries 154

Philadelphia Cheesesteaks 156

Philadelphia Distilleries 158

b.good 160

The Olde Bar 162

Wm. Mulherin's Sons 164

Rival Bros. Coffee Roasters 166

Kennett Square 168

Revolutionary Hospitality 170

Fante's Kitchen Shop 172

Mac Mart 174

Wok'N Walk Tours of Chinatown 176

Ferry Market 178

Philadelphia Restaurant Week 180

Beer Gardens 182

Wawa 184

Townsend 186

bāo • logy 188

Laurel 190

BYOBs 192

Private Dining Rooms 194

We Heart 13th Street Restaurant Group 196

Garces Group 198

Starr Restaurants 200

Restaurants A-Z 202

Appendix 209

Zahav. Photo by Alexandra Hawkins

INTRODUCTION

As I began writing *Unique Eats and Eateries of Philadelphia*, it became clear that Philadelphians and visitors were hungry for a book about local restaurants. This book tells the stories behind the city's restaurants—from the charming engagement story of two chocolatiers to the tale of a birthday party for a beloved ninety-year-old customer, from a storage closet that became a restaurant to a signless speakeasy in Chinatown. To be included in this book, the restaurants needed not only a good story but also good food. So readers who eat up the stories will also be eating well. Every restaurant mentioned is a solid representative of Philadelphia's vibrant restaurant scene.

I heard some of the stories while handling public relations for Philadelphia restaurants for nearly three decades. I uncovered other stories by interviewing chefs and restaurant owners; scouring websites, articles, and videos; talking to food writers and quizzing friends and strangers about their favorite places to eat; and by seemingly endless eating. It was always exciting when I unearthed a good story.

After writing my first book, *100 Things to Do in Philadelphia Before You Die*, some people joked that I should call this book *100 Places to Eat in Philadelphia*, but it includes far more than one hundred restaurants. Readers will also find tips on how to snag reservations at trendy restaurants as well as an insider's scoop on dishes to taste, things to see, and food- and drink-related things to do.

I'd like to thank June Baker, copy editor extraordinaire, who went far above and beyond my expectations; Rachel Baker, a tough but talented writer; and David Baker, who not only edited the copy but also had the enviable task of being my research assistant (i.e., dining partner). While that included delightful dining adventures and serving as designated drinker, many of his meals grew cold as I staged pictures and soon he'll have the less glamorous task of lugging around boxes of books.

I'd also like to thank: Karoline Adler and Jon Auerbach; Cari Feiler Bender; Francine Bloch; Richard Bookbinder; Jake Buganski; Laura Burkhardt; Alethia Calbeck; Rita Caplan; Christina Cassidy; Shelley Chamberlain; Danielle Cohn; Marilyn Frank and David Feldman; Sharla Feldscher; Sam Gordon and Susan Gross; Sheila Hess; Holly Keefe, Action Wellness/Dining Out for Life; Nina Kelly and the Chester County Conference & Visitors Bureau; Ellen Horowitz Matz; Jay Nachman; Rick Nichols; Megan York Parker; Clare Pelino and Profile Public Relations; Devon Perry and Visit South Jersey; Donna Schorr, Cara Schneider and Visit Philadelphia; Ellen Soloff and Mural Arts Philadelphia; the Philadelphia Convention and Visitors Bureau; Naomi Starobin and Ed von Stein; Alex Tewfik; and Jessica Willingham and the Valley Forge Tourism and Convention Board.

I'd also like to thank the chefs and restaurants who shared their stories, the managers and publicists who shared their time, and the organizations that gave their ideas.

Kudos to the talented staff at Reedy Press who published *100 Things to Do in Philadelphia Before You Die* and this second book. And thanks to those who supported the first book, including the Philadelphia Convention & Visitors Bureau, Comcast, Visit Philadelphia, Select Greater Philadelphia, and the many bookstores, hotels, gift shops and, of course, the readers.

I appreciate the support of my parents Sharon Bohm Levy and Marvin Levy, and my son, Adam Baker, as well as their sales acumen and overwhelming enthusiasm and thanks to my extended family and friends.

TEN TIPS FOR GETTING RESERVATIONS AT PHILADELPHIA'S TOP RESTAURANTS

1. Be flexible. Saturday at 7:00 p.m. is the most popular time to dine. Try earlier or later or, better yet, on a weeknight when it'll be quieter and you'll get better service.

2. Try Open Table, but be aware that not every available slot is listed. Restaurants don't post the most popular time slots (such as Saturday at 7:00 p.m.).

3. Call. Sometimes openings aren't listed on Open Table.

4. Ask if the restaurant has a waiting list and will call if someone cancels.

5. Ask about walk-ins. Make reservations at your second choice restaurant at 7:30 p.m. Walk in to your first choice an hour before. If they have a table, you're good. Just remember to cancel your later reservations. Otherwise, you have a backup plan.

6. Sit at the bar, where seats are first come, first served. You can almost always get the full menu at the bar, and it's fun.

7. Ask the restaurant for their rules. It takes a year to get reservations at Talula's Table, and they open their reservation book to the exact numerical day at 7:00 a.m. Most restaurants aren't so extreme, but find out when they open the reservation book for the month and call then.

8. Instead of calling with a particular date/time, ask the restaurant when they have availability and take it.

9. Sign up for the restaurant's e-newsletter and watch for announcements about openings.

10. Follow chefs and restaurants on social media. They'll often post if they have a cancellation or opening.

UNIQUE EATS AND EATERIES

OF

PHILADELPHIA

Chocolate with a mission

John Doyle and Kira Baker started a chocolate-making company called John & Kira's in 2002. Just a few months later *Gourmet* magazine called it "their favorite chocolate" and put it on the cover of the Valentine's Day issue. When the magazine's fact checker called to confirm that John and Kira were a married couple, they weren't, but John asked them to leave in the reference. When the preview copy of the issue arrived, John handed it to Kira at the dinner table with an engagement ring taped inside.

After fifteen years in the chocolate-making business, the couple sold the company to their old friend Christopher Dal Piaz, who was committed to continuing their socially conscious mission. The company, still called John & Kira's after its founders, sources ingredients for its chocolate from urban high school gardens, small family farms, and employee-owned cooperatives producing chocolates with a clear, fresh flavor.

John & Kira's is known for its whimsically shaped confections such as striped honey caramel bees and polka-dotted lady bugs, as well as Urban Garden Chocolate bars, flavored with mint, Guajillo chili peppers, and rosemary grown in urban farms in Philadelphia, Chicago, and Washington, D.C. John & Kira's supplies the plants to urban schools, buys what is harvested, and gives five percent of sales back to support educational gardening programs for city youth. That is chocolate you can feel good about eating.

800-747-4808
johnandkiras.com

Top: Bee-shaped chocolates by John & Kira's.

Above left: Urban Garden Chocolate Bar made with mint grown on urban farms.

Above right: John Boyle & Kira Baker-Doyle.

Other standout confectionaries in Philadelphia:

Aurora Grace Chocolates

auroragracechocolates.com

Artisanal, handcrafted chocolate bonbons, plus macarons, bars, and baked goods.

Éclat Chocolate

24 S. High St., West Chester, PA, 610-692-5206, eclatchocolate.com

Chocolatier Christopher Curtin honed his skills at chocolate houses in Belgium, Switzerland, France, Japan, and Germany, where he was the first American awarded the honor of German Master Pastry Chef and Chocolatier.

Mueller Chocolate Co.

Reading Terminal Market (see page 148), 51 N. 12th St., 215-922-6164

muellerschocolate.com

A family-owned shop known for its chocolate-covered candies and anatomically correct chocolate body parts, including hearts and lungs, which made it into *Ripley's Believe It Or Not.*

Sciasa Confections (see page 178)

sciasciaconfections.com

It WILL give you goosebumps

It's hard to say which causes more goosebumps. Is it the taste and beauty of Chris Kearse's food or the story of how he became an award-winning chef? Trained under Laurent Gras and other big-name chefs, including Thomas Keller and Grant Achatz, Kearse is now winning awards for his restaurant, Will BYOB.

Like Achatz, the award-winning chef/owner of Alinea who survived mouth cancer, Kearse was shaped by his life experiences. He says he was born to cook, and by the time he was in high school, he had digested hours of food TV, devoured hundreds of cookbooks, and regularly prepared dinner for his parents and seven siblings in his home in suburban Philadelphia.

But the road that got him there was treacherous. Shortly before his sixteenth birthday, Kearse was involved in an automobile accident. He was bedridden for more than a year, undergoing thirty-five surgeries to rebuild the lower portion of his face. He dropped nearly one hundred pounds and had to relearn to talk and eventually to eat. While he retained his sense of taste, Kearse lost his sense of smell. He says he remembers the smell of rosemary, truffle, pineapple, and other foods and knows how much salt to add because he does it all day every day.

Kearse went on to graduate as valedictorian from The Restaurant School at Walnut Hill College, impressing his classmates with his drive and work ethic. His perseverance led him to stints with top-name chefs at The French Laundry in California and Chicago's Tru and Alinea before bringing the techniques he learned home to Philadelphia in 2008.

He made his mark at Lacroix and Pumpkin before realizing his dream of opening his own restaurant, Will BYOB. The restaurant's

Top right: Hazelnut financier with soft chocolate ganache and grapefruit sorbet. Photo by Jason Hook.

Above left: Chef Chris Kearse. Photo by Jason Hook.

Above right: Mackerel Crudo, dashi ponzu, winter radishes, caramelized white soy. Photo by Jason Hook.

name is a perfect fit because by a happy coincidence that old saying "where there's a will, there's a way" not only fits Kearse's story perfectly but it's also his middle name and what his family calls him. BYOB stands for Bring Your Own Bottle (see page 192).

At Will BYOB, Kearse creates modern French-inspired cuisine. Each dish is like a tiny gem, painstakingly constructed and *almost* too beautiful to eat. That will has brought Kearse two nominations from the James Beard Foundation and accolades from *Philadelphia* magazine and starchefs.com.

His petite BYOB can be found on trendy East Passyunk, a thriving restaurant row in the heart of South Philadelphia.

1911 E. Passyunk Ave., 215-271-7683

willbyob.com

DANTE & LUIGI'S CORONA DI FERRO

Almost dying for a good meal

There are restaurants that people are dying to try, and then there are restaurants where people almost died trying them.

In 1981, after Philip "Chicken Man" Testa was killed by a bomb under his porch, "Little Nicky" Scarfo took over the crime business. In 1987, Little Nicky, who was known to be ruthless and hot-tempered, was convicted of racketeering and murder and sentenced to fifty-five years in prison. He tried to continue running the business by using his son, Nicodemo S. Scarfo, as a conduit. The arrangement didn't work out so well. On Halloween Night 1989, a man in a Batman mask walked into Dante & Luigi's Corona di Ferro, approached Nicodemo's table, pulled a gun out of a trick or treat bag, and shot Nicodemo about half a dozen times. Miraculously, Nicodemo survived the shooting, but a jury got him in 2015, when he was sent to prison for thirty years.

The restaurant is a survivor, too, having opened more than a hundred years ago. Michael DiRocco opened the traditional Italian restaurant in a Victorian house. When Italian immigrants arrived in Philadelphia, they used to head straight to the restaurant for jobs and

DON'T MISS: La Veranda is the site of another bungled mob hit. In 1992, Rosario Bellocchi found his way into the restaurant kitchen and held a sawed-off shotgun to the head of Biagi Andornetto, the restaurant's pizza chef. It misfired, and Bellocchi ended up chasing Andornetto through the restaurant. Andonetto escaped and headed to Italy. The would-be hit man became a government witness.

Left: Dante & Luigi's Corona di Ferro.

Right: Dante & Luigi's to-die-for lasagna.

a room in the boarding house upstairs. Its original name, Corona di Ferro, was changed in the 1930s when DiRocco left the restaurant to his sons, Dante and Luigi. They ran the restaurant together, and it reportedly become a gangster hangout.

In 1996, the restaurant changed hands, and the new owners totally renovated the building and changed almost everything else except the name and type of cuisine. Current owners, Michael and Connie LaRussa, serve Italian dishes based on the recipes that Michael's mother and grandmother brought over from Sicily, including the Italian red gravy (sauce) that's slow cooked for six hours. Signature dishes, including the Osso Buco, Sweet Breads, and Homemade Cheese Gnocchi, still attract celebs. Former Vice President Joe Biden has a house account at Dante & Luigi's and periodically dines there. The LaRussas prefer to dwell on the big names it attracts from the White House rather than the big house.

Dante & Luigi's
762 S. 10th St., 215-922-9501
danteandluigis.com

La Veranda
Penn's Landing, Pier 3, 215-351-1898
laverandapier3.com

GRAN CAFFÈ L'AQUILA

Tragedy in Italy brings triumph to Philadelphia

Gran Caffè L'Aquila calls itself the "most authentic Italian cafe in America," and perhaps it is judging from the Italian expats who frequent the place. It had a prime location on the Piazza Duomo in L'Aquila in the Abruzzo region of Italy, where it won Italy's coveted "Cafe of the Year" award. In 2007, the cafe and much of the town were felled by an earthquake.

Instead of rebuilding in the central Italian city, Riccardo Longo persuaded the owners to reopen in his adopted city of Philadelphia, home to one of the largest Abruzzese populations in the world outside of Abruzzo.

The fortes of the three owners—wine, gelato, coffees—are reflected in the restaurant. Chef Stefano Biasini won the Italian gelato championship and International Press World Championship. Michele Morelli was named an ambassador of Italian coffee and has served coffee to world leaders. Longo's family owned a vineyard in Italy, and he has studied the cuisine and wines of Italy's twenty regions.

Gran Caffè L'Aquila is buzzing all day serving classic Italian coffee using beans roasted on-site and traditional Italian pastries in the morning and Italian wines in the evening. In between, the restaurant serves both lunch and dinner. The authentic Italian cuisine includes a weekly tasting menu focused on the food and wine of one of the cities in Italy and can be topped off with sweet—or savory—gelato

> **DON'T MISS:** The vertical tasting of gelato. The tasting typically includes heaping spoonfuls of mixed berry, Amarena cherry, zabaglione, pistachio, and dark chocolate.

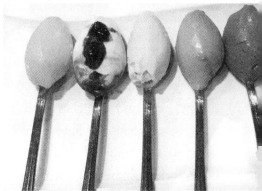

Top: Owners Chef Stefano Biasini, Riccardo Longo, and Michele Morelli.

Above left: Carbonara with pancetta gelato.

Above right: Vertical gelato tasting. Photo by Rachel Baker.

made on-site in their own gelato kitchen. The long menu can be a bit overwhelming, but the servers, who sport fedoras, seem to revel in explaining it all in great depth.

The restaurant has two bars—one serving cocktails and Italian tapas and the other specializing in Italian wines, including Amaro and Grappa. The restaurant, which opened in 2015, has already earned two Awards of Excellence from *Wine Spectator*.

1716 Chestnut St., 215-568-5600

grancaffelaquila.com

Reconnecting generations

Frieda's website clearly states that it's not a coffee shop, bakery, restaurant, community center, or gallery. In fact, it's all that and much more. It's a space designed to make lives richer by reconnecting generations over food, activities, and conversation.

It's the brainchild of Le Cordon Bleu-trained chef David Wong and his business partner, Thomas Steinborn, who named the space after his grandmother. Many of the employees are retirees who still need, or want, to work.

Frieda's breakfast and lunch menus feature simple, healthy fare made from locally sourced, sustainable products. Gluten-free, vegan, and vegetarian options are marked on the menu. Community dinners, teas, and brunches are scheduled several times a month.

The schedule also includes lessons in several languages, crafts (knitting and drawing), and other interests, such as social media, books, bridge, canasta, cooking, backgammon, and films. Not convinced yet? Then you can set up your own activity. They encourage people to point their noses toward each other rather than a screen, and it's working. It's not unusual to see a diverse group with a fifty-year age span playing mah jongg or sharing cheddar rosemary scones.

As if the mission wasn't welcoming enough, big windows and works by local artists keep the space vibrant and bright even on cloudy days. New white walls go about three-quarters of the way to the ceiling, creating a facade that partially exposes the beautiful, rustic bones of the building and giving a peek of what the building

DON'T MISS: Frieda's signature almond cake is made by a pastry chef who is old enough to be your grandmother.

Top: David Wong (behind counter) at Frieda. Photo by Kendon Photography.

Above left: Afternoon tea at Frieda. Photo by Jorge Monedero.

Above right: Gail Caruso, jam maker at Frieda. Photo by Jorge Monedero.

might have looked like in yesteryear. The older walls have stood the test of time, lending great character to the interior. The new and old work together to create something stronger than either would be alone and perhaps serving as a metaphor for the activity taking place within the warm space.

320 Walnut St., 215-600-1291

friedaforgenerations.com

11

Philadelphia's oldest continuously operating tavern

McGillin's swung open its doors in 1860, the year Abe Lincoln was elected president. The historic tavern's long, storied history is filled with celebrities, ghosts, and a tale of survival through not only the economic recession but also the Great Depression and even Prohibition. Through it all, McGillin's has been owned by only two families: Catherine and William McGillin, who raised their thirteen children upstairs, and the current owners, the Spaniak/Mullins family, who have passed it down through three generations.

It was originally called Bell in Hand Tavern, but regulars nicknamed it McGillin's, and the name stuck. After William's death, Catherine, a tough bird who didn't allow rowdiness, ran the establishment, surviving Prohibition by serving food, including free baked potatoes, and "tea" upstairs.

In 1958, the McGillin children sold the bar to brothers and experienced barkeeps Henry Spaniak and Joe Shepaniak. (That's not a mistake. The brothers actually spelled their names differently.) Keeping it in the family, Henry's daughter, Mary Ellen Spaniak Mullins, and her husband, Chris Mullins, Sr., have run the restaurant since 1993, and the legacy of hospitality continues with their son, Christopher Mullins, Jr., representing the family's third generation to manage the historic tavern.

The history hangs right on the walls at the classic English-looking pub, with a beamed ceiling, tall windows, dark paneling, and a working

DON'T MISS. Free homemade soup from an old-fashioned self-serve kettle with every lunch and the six beer sampler, including mugs of McGillin's house beers, plus three local craft brews.

Top left: McGillin's interior. Photo by Thomas Robert Clarke.

Above left: The McGillin family.

Above right: Chris Mullins, Sr., Mary Ellen Mullins and Christopher Mullins, Jr. Photo by Thomas Robert Clarke.

fireplace. The walls are decked with old liquor licenses, musical instruments, varsity banners, aged newspaper clips, historic photos, and signs from bygone Philadelphia stores and restaurants. Spottings of professional athletes, musicians, movie and TV stars, comedians, and other celebs are not uncommon at this iconic Philadelphia bar.

McGillin's serves thirty local craft beers on tap, including three house beers made by Stoudts Brewing in Adamstown, and hearty comfort food. The tavern's patrons get younger as the day gets later. The lunch crowd includes office workers, politicos from nearby City Hall, conventioneers, and, especially during the winter holidays when it's decorated to the hilt, families. Millennials flock there in the evening for beer and food specials and because they know that more couples have met at McGillin's than anywhere else in the city.

1310 Drury St., 215-735-5562
mcgillins.com

One of the nation's first urban farms

*B*lanche Gets A Job is a beautifully illustrated children's book about a cat that finds a home and a job at Food for People Farm. The book isn't entirely fictitious. A cat named Blanche was a beloved resident of Greensgrow Farms. Thanks to her bird-chasing skills, Blanche was named Integrated Pest Management Specialist at the farm. The mischievous feline was even named employee of the year several times, even though she was often late for meetings. The book's author, Mary Seton Corboy, was the founder, chief idea officer, and visionary behind Greensgrow, a nationally recognized leader in urban farming and agriculture.

Besides her affection for Blanche, Corboy was known for her interest in healthy food, love of physical labor, and desire to give back. Although Corboy succumbed to cancer in 2016, her passions inspired a long-lasting legacy. In 1997, she and Tom Sereduk, her business partner, created the farm on a former trash-covered factory site that took up a whole city block in Kensington. Their venture started as a hydroponic lettuce farm and grew into much more. It now harvests more than twenty types of vegetables. Corboy accomplished her dream of feeding, nourishing, and employing the community. Greensgrow Farms has now become a community hub.

Each year Greensgrow Farms produces more than two thousand pounds of fresh produce in its large raised beds, a six-thousand-square-foot greenhouse, hydroponic beds, and smart containers. The urban farm has a thriving retail nursery, a community-supported agriculture (CSA) program called Greensgrow Farm Share, a farm stand, educational programming, and a mini-menagerie. While Blanche has used up her nine lives, the farm is still home to several beloved two- and four-legged creatures, including Milkshake the

Top right: Blanche. Photo by Bryn Ashburn.

Above left: Mary Seton Corboy. Photo by Jennifer Kourkounis.

Above right: Greensgrow. Photo by Bryn Ashburn.

pig, Ping the duck, chickens, turtles, beehives, and the non-legged residents of a koi pond.

Greensgrow has a community kitchen in a church a few blocks from the farm, and a second site called Greensgrow West has a garden center, greenhouse, and chickens in West Philadelphia. For those who can't get to one of the sites, Greensgrow has mobile market trucks that bring fresh, healthy food items at affordable prices to underserved and economically disadvantaged parts of Philadelphia.

2501 E. Cumberland St., 215-427-2780
greensgrow.org

A safe haven

For privacy, it would be hard to find a better spot than South Camac, a cobblestone lane barely wide enough for a car. Add the tunnels running beneath it and you have the ideal locale for clandestine activities.

The tiny building on the tiny street has been a safe haven for gays since the 1920s and before that very likely for former slaves on the road to freedom. The bar's wine cellar appears to be part of a tunnel system running through the neighborhood, and rumor has it that the building was once part of the Underground Railroad. As Philadelphia was a major player in the resistance network, this claim has been deemed highly likely. Some believe that the bricked-up archway may have been a passage to shelter, food, and hiding for those seeking freedom. While the Underground Railroad was often not actually "underground," the quiet, petite street is ideal for missions requiring secrecy.

By the late nineteenth and early twentieth century, South Camac Street was home to literary, art, and advertising clubs as well as tea rooms and restaurants. It's said that during Prohibition the street was also lined with speakeasies, another potential use for those tunnels. The building now housing Tavern on Camac has gone through many owners and name changes but has consistently been a gay bar since 1927, making it home to the oldest continuously operating gay bar in Philadelphia.

Many colorful characters have crossed the threshold, including well-known actors working at nearby theaters and Mary the Hat, a longtime coat checker known for her favorite accessory. Rumor has it that she lived across the tiny street, and when it rained, she called a cab and paid two dollars to go in the back door, slide across the backseat, and get out on the other side so that she wouldn't get wet.

Left: Camac Street. Photo by Rachel Baker.

Right: The tunnel beneath Tavern on Camac is used as a wine cellar.

Her driver, a regular at the bar, reportedly would then give the two dollars to her doorman, who would return it to her the next morning.

Today, Tavern on Camac is a restaurant, piano bar, and nightclub with good food, great drinks, and a friendly, welcoming vibe.

243 S. Camac St., 215-545-1102

tavernoncamac.com

More restaurants with possible connections to the Underground Railroad:

Bistro Romano

120 Lombard St., 215-925-8880

bistroromano.com

Fitzwater Station

264 Canal St., Phoenixville, PA, 610-933-1420

fitzwaterstation.com

A tale, with nary a tail

Rich Landau and Kate Jacoby's story has all the makings of a good tale—a romance, a few challenges, a mission, and a happy ending. What it doesn't have is a tail, as it's a saga with absolutely no animal parts.

In 1994 Landau ran a ten-seat counter inside a health food store in suburban Philadelphia where Jacoby was a customer. When he expanded into the storefront next door, she took a summer job as a hostess. Things began to heat up for Landau and Jacoby as well as for the restaurant, which moved into an even bigger space two doors down. Then the summer ended, and Jacoby left for a year in France. After six months, she was back, working alongside Landau once again.

By 2006, the couple was ready to take on Center City with a larger space and a liquor license for their restaurant, Horizon. The cuisine had evolved from dishes focusing on protein substitutes to dishes that looked at vegetables in new ways—using such techniques as fermenting, char grilling, pickling, and smoking to bring out the flavors, textures, and colors. The trend toward small plates meant diners no longer expected a big protein dish paired with a vegetable, and people were becoming interested in the connection between food and health, artisanal foods, locally grown products, and community-supported agriculture (CSA) programs.

The growing interest in vegetarian dining enabled them to take another big step in 2011. They closed Horizon and opened their flagship restaurant, Vedge, in a beautiful mansion in the city with a noteworthy bar and exceptional wine list. They call it a vegetable restaurant rather than vegan because it's about the cuisine, not the lifestyle. With Vedge, they have earned several James Beard nominations and accolades from *Travel + Leisure* and *Food &*

Left: Kate Jacoby and Rich Landau. Photo by Yoni Nimrod.

Right: Vedge's fancy radishes with avocado and smoked tamari. Photo by Yoni Nimrod.

Wine. GQ called Vedge one of the best restaurants in the country, vegetarian or otherwise.

In 2014, they opened V Street where they interpret street food from around the world. Three years later they expanded into the space next door with Wiz Kid, a fast-casual restaurant that allows them to embrace Philadelphia's reputation as a cheesesteak town with their version of a mushroom-centric cheesesteak, and in 2018 they opened Fancy Radish in Washington, D.C. Now that's a happy ending.

Vedge

1221 Locust St., 215-320-7500

vedgerestaurant.com

V Street

126 S. 19th St., 215-278-7943

vstreetfood.com

Wiz Kid

124 S. 19th St., 267-639-5764

wizkidfood.com

Cheu Fishtown. Photo by Danya Henninger, Imagic Digital.

More Vegetarian/Vegan Restaurants:

Bar Bombón
133 S. 18th St., 267-606-6612, barbombon.com

Vegan restaurant featuring Puerto Rico foods with a twist. By Nicole Marquis.

Blue Sage Vegetarian Grille
727 2nd Street Pike, Southampton, PA, 215-942-8888
bluesagevegetariangrille.com

Vegan fare in a pleasant atmosphere in Bucks County.

Charlie was a sinner
131 S. 13th St., 267-758-5372, charliewasasinner.com

Vegan drinks and small plates in a hip atmosphere. By Nicole Marquis.

Citizens Bank Park
One Citizens Bank Way, mlb.com/phillies

Named to the People for the Ethical Treatment of Animals (PETA) list of vegetarian-friendly Major League Baseball ballparks year after year.

Cheu Noodle Bar, Cheu Fishtown, Bing Bing Dim Sum (see page 78)
cheunoodlebar.com

Dishes that are vegetarian or can be made vegetarian are marked on menus.

Front Street Cafe
1253 N. Front St., 215-515-3073, frontstreetcafe.net

Vegetarian-friendly with local plant-based farm-to-table and organic ingredients and a variety of vegan options.

Goldie (see page 48)
goldiefalafel.com

Casual falafel bar with fries and tehina shakes. Vegan and kosher.

Left: Goldie's Tehina Shake. Photo by Michael Persico.

Right: Goldie. Photo by Michael Persico.

Hip City Veg
121 S. Broad St., 267-296-9001
214 S. 40th St., 267-244-4342
127 S. 18th St., 215-278-7605
301 S. Christopher Columbus Blvd.
hipcityveg.com
Vegan fast-casual by Nicole Marquis.

Mama's Vegetarian
18 S. 20th St., 215-751-0477
No-frills kosher eatery serving mostly falafel and hummus. Mostly vegan.

Miss Rachel's Pantry (see page 38)
missrachelspantry.com
A vegan and kosher BYOB. Catering and classes available.

P.S. & Co
1706 Locust St., 215-985-1706, puresweets.com
Casual vegan restaurant serving 100 percent organic products.

Sprig & Vine
450 Union Square Dr., New Hope, PA, 215-693-1427, sprigandvine.com
Cozy vegan BYOB in New Hope.

Vientiane Café (see page 32)
vientiane-cafe.com
Offers many vegetarian and vegan dishes.

A tasty time capsule

The rules at Palizzi Social Club make it seem gimmicky until you experience the butterflies in your stomach when waiting to see if you'll get in. If you're lucky enough to make the cut, at the end of the evening you'll leave highly satisfied with the excellent meal and expertly mixed cocktails, and possibly even with three or four new best friends.

Palizzi Social Club opened in 1918 as a place for expats of the Italian town of Vasto in Southern Abruzzo to eat, drink, celebrate, and make deals. It was named for the town's most famous resident, Filippo Palizzi, a painter. Eventually, membership was opened to immigrants from elsewhere in Italy.

By the time Joey Baldino took over the club, the old-school neon sign that indicated when it was open rarely flickered on. Baldino, a well-respected chef of Zeppoli BYOB in Collingswood, New Jersey, is a third-generation owner and president of the club. He revitalized the club and worked with the board to rewrite the charter to open membership to the public. You still need a membership, but you no longer have to be from Vasto or even Italy. It's still not easy to get in, as just six months after opening, the club was named the Fourth Best New Restaurant in America by *Bon Appétit* and was so overwhelmed with membership requests that it suspended new memberships, hopefully only temporarily.

If you don't have a membership, you can still get through the knobless front door if you have a friend who is a member. Each member may take up to three guests, but they have to be the sort that you'd take to your mom's house. That's one of the rules.

It's not the exclusivity, though, that makes it enticing. It's actually the inclusivity. Once you sit down at the bar, you are treated like the regular that you want to become. Then the food and drinks

Left: Palizzi Social Club Interior. Photo by Jason Varney.

Right: Cuisine at Palizzi Social Club. Photo by Jason Varney.

start coming. The menu is based on Baldino's family recipes, such as a Caesar Salad, Spaghetti with Crabs, and Brasciole so good that the bartender swears she regularly sees diners crossing themselves and apologizing to their dead grandmothers for preferring Baldino's version.

Speaking of grandmothers, you may feel that you're dining in an ancestor's home with the Formica bar top, vinyl barstools, fake wood paneling, and black-and-white photos, but somehow it all works. That, and '50s dinner club music (think Frank Sinatra), including weekly live music that doesn't overpower the small room, all add to the welcoming feeling.

Another rule is that your membership will be revoked if you write a review of Palizzi Social Club. So, just to be clear, this is a description but not a review. I want to go back. Soon!

1408 S.12th St.

palizzisocial.com

The scoop on America's oldest ice cream shop

In 1861, Lewis Dubois Bassett, a Quaker school teacher and farmer living in Salem, New Jersey, made his first pint of ice cream using a mule-turned churn in his backyard. Today, his great-great grandson runs the business, which has made thousands of ice cream lovers happy, including former President Barack Obama.

Bassett opened his first ice cream parlor in 1885 at 5th and Market Streets, in the heart of Center City Philadelphia. About seven years later Bassetts moved a few blocks west to Reading Terminal Market (see page 148) making it the oldest merchant in the market. It is still in the same location and the marble counters are the originals.

Over the years, Bassetts has created more than one hundred super premium flavors, including such oddities as yellow tomato and borscht (the latter for former Soviet Premier Nikita Khrushchev in 1959).

Today, Bassetts offers more than forty flavors of ice cream and sorbet. Most are gluten free. Besides Reading Terminal Market, Bassetts can now be found in restaurants, ice cream parlors, country clubs, hotels, and supermarkets, and it is also served by caterers. The ice cream is available throughout the Philadelphia region, in major cities across the United States, and as far away as South Korea and China.

While the ice cream making is no longer powered by mules, it is still in the family. Lewis Dubois Bassett's great-great-great grandsons, representing the sixth generation, are learning the business.

Reading Terminal Market
51 N.12th St., 215-925-4315
bassettsicecream.com

Top: Bassetts Ice Cream.

Above left: First Bassetts Ice Cream Parlor on Market Street.

Above right: Roger Bassett, Eric Bassett, Alex Bassett Strange, Michael Strange at Bassetts in Reading Terminal Market.

DON'T MISS: The vanilla ice cream. The same recipe, calling for Madagascar bourbon vanilla, has been followed for more than eight decades.

Mind your manners at the "World's Best Bar"

When you hear about this speakeasy in Chinatown, with its impressive selection of high-end liquors, many rules, and list of 1,600 banned patrons, you'll think that it's as mysterious and eccentric as its one-named proprietor, Lê.

But really it's about being unique and demanding respect. Lê had a vision—opening a cocktail bar serving high-end liquors not often found in bars. He traveled the country trying to find just the right city for his vision. Luckily, he found it in Philadelphia's Chinatown (see page 90), which has a winning combination of cheap rent and close proximity to his family. He thought his bar would attract patrons from the many ethnic restaurants in the neighborhood, but as it turns out it's the other way around. The bar is the destination.

Hop Sing Laundromat, which *Condé Nast Traveler* dubbed "one of the best bars in the world," doesn't have a sign. What it does have is a lot of rules, such as no photos, and a dress code—no flip-flops, shorts, or baseball caps. On the bar's fifth anniversary in 2017, Lê announced that sneakers, which were previously forbidden, would be permitted.

But—there's a method to his madness, which is perhaps . . . genius. The crazy name of the bar is from a character on *Bonanza*, an old TV show. Since there is no sign, the bar is a mindful destination—not a place binge drinkers wander into looking for a cheap PBR (Pabst Blue Ribbon). Lê, the only one who has a key to the door, wants

DON'T MISS: The Nevermore (Smooth Amber Gin, Patrón Citrónge, Vietnamese coffee and cream), which was rarely ordered until a local food critic tried it and praised the unlikely combination.

Top: Interior. Photo by Robert Neroni. Courtesy of Hop Sing Laundromat.

Above left: The entrance. Find the black iron gate and ring the bell. Only ring once as impatient ringers are often denied entrance. Photo by Irene Levy Baker.

Above right: Drinks at Hop Sing Laundromat. Photo by Robert Neroni. Courtesy of Hop Sing Laundromat.

guests who understand what he's created with his meticulously chosen decor, brick-exposed walls, nickel-covered bar, and esoteric liquors. Why no selfies? Like the widely spaced tables that's for guests' privacy. The dress code? When people told him that a dress code would never fly in Philadelphia, it became a challenge.

The dress code and the rules keep it classy. That line down the street that Lê never expected? Curse about how long you waited and you may never get in, but if you do and then take a photo or drink too much, you're likely to get kicked out or even banned for life.

1029 Race St.

hopsinglaundromat.com

The closet of their dreams

Marina de Oliveira and her husband, Chris D'Ambro, "adopted" Southwark, a gastropub in Queen Village, in February 2016. Seven months later the couple gave birth to Ambra, the restaurant they really wanted. Southwark is delightful in its own right, with a charming patio and beautifully presented food, but Ambra is their favorite child.

When they purchased the property, the real attraction was the empty storage closet off the kitchen. That's where de Oliveira and D'Ambro planned to open their dream restaurant. Chris transformed the closet into a rustic sixteen-seater with wood, metal, and concrete accents and walls decorated with illuminated boxes draped in fabric, with the help of his brother, Joseph D'Ambro, who handbuilt almost everything.

The new baby was named Ambra, the original family name of the D'Ambro brothers. Many years ago their grandfather changed his last name from Ambra to D'Ambro to distance himself from his brothers, who ran a less-than-savory business. Chris and Joseph, who get along better than their ancestors, use their grandfather's adopted name, D'Ambro, and the restaurant goes by the family's original name, Ambra.

Before opening Ambra, D'Ambro studied at the Culinary Institute of America; interned at Vetri Cucina (see page 146), where he worked with Marc Vetri, Michael Solomonov (see page 48), and Joey Baldino (see page 22); and cooked at Talula's Table (see page 86). This is not the first time that Ambro and de Oliveira have worked together. They met when they were both on the opening team of Talula's Garden (see page 200), and just before returning to Philadelphia to open Ambra, they were coworkers at Flora's Field Kitchen, an organic farm in San José del Cabo, Mexico.

Left: Ambra interior. Photo by Joseph D'Ambro.

Right: Beetroot cured Swordfish Bresola. Photo by Casey Robinson.

At Ambra, diners are seated at half-hour intervals and served a nine-course prix fixe menu with optional wine pairings. The tiny restaurant is known for pampering diners with personal service. Such an intimate experience is possible because the two restaurants share a kitchen and liquor license. Ambra is the couple's raison d'être, and it may well be yours too.

Ambra
705 S. 4th St., 267-858-9232
ambraphilly.com

Southwark
701 S. 4th St., 267-930-8538
southwarkrestaurant.com

DON'T MISS: Southwark's charming 18-seat patio. With its tiny white lights, herbs, and tomatoes, it is a delightful place to sip craft cocktails and eat dinner.

Quirky, but quaint

Maria and Marc Farnese named their charming BYOB after the proprietor of their favorite trattoria in Italy. When they went back to Italy years later, they were disappointed to find that it had been modernized beyond recognition. Nonetheless their tribute to the Italian trattoria has survived for more than twenty-seven years. They opened their restaurant long before East Passyunk was ground zero for hip restaurants and review-site-addicted foodies. Mr. Martino's seems frozen in time, but diners will not be disappointed with this romantic jewel box serving what the couple describes as "peasant" food which leaves diners feeling satisfied, well fed, and pampered.

Marc, a soft-spoken former antiques dealer, and Maria, a former fabric designer, run Mr. Martino's with the help of warm and knowledgeable servers. The small payroll allows them the luxury to open only on Friday, Saturday, and Sunday nights, but the lack of manpower means they spend all week preparing for the weekends, and when Maria, a self-taught cook, broke her arm or when they want to take a vacation, they have to close.

The fifty-seat restaurant was a hardware store before the couple transformed it into a cozy, antique-filled trattoria, and there are still hints of its former life, such as the hardware store's name in the tile foyer floor and the big front windows, though they now sport a quirky tableau of a table and chairs with two decades' worth of old reservations books strewn below. The Farneses have lovingly maintained the tin ceiling, wooden entrance wall, and bar and added

TIP: When you call to make reservations, you'll have to leave a message. If you don't hear back, you're good to go.

Top right: Pasta at Mr. Martino's Trattoria. Photo by Irene Levy Baker.

Above left: Mr. Martino's Exterior. Photo by Irene Levy Baker.

Above right: Mr. Martino's interior. Photo by Sue Goldstein.

off-beat accents, such as a headless statue, family photos, and antique oil paintings in gilt frames, making it as warm as the bosomy hugs of your favorite aunt.

Maria works alone in the kitchen on a six-burner stove, so this isn't the place to dine if you're on a tight schedule. Service isn't speedy, but it's worth the wait, and once you taste the sauces on her pastas, balsamic chicken, octopus, and broccoli rabe, the large bread basket will finally make sense. You'll want to clean your plate and will need the bread to sop up every last drop. If you have a dog at home waiting for a doggie bag, he's going to be disappointed. But you won't be!

1646 E. Passyunk Ave., 215-755-0663

Started in a backyard tent

In the 1980s, Daovy Phanthavong, a refugee from the communist regime in Laos, started cooking Lao dishes for friends at her new home in West Philadelphia. Her table became a place for refugees to hang out with friends and get an authentic meal. She was such a good cook that soon her friends were bringing *their* friends. Word spread and soon students from the nearby universities and others from the community were clamoring to taste her homestyle pad thai and curries.

Daovy loved sharing her homeland's cuisine and culture with her neighbors, and soon the crowd overwhelmed the house at 45th and Sansom and overflowed onto tables in the backyard. Her husband, Phoxay Sidara, covered the tables with blue tarp, and everyone called the secret restaurant the "blue tent" or the "backyard spot." People lined up for $3 plates of pad thai and curries cooked to order with the help of the couple's daughters, Manorack and Sunny. Former refugees, neighbors, students, and a motorcycle gang, along with the family's dogs, cats, and even a chicken named "Chicken," broke bread together under the blue tent. The friendly scene came to an abrupt end, however, when a policeman noticed all the cars and inquired about a license. Afterward, neighbors and students still came begging Daovy to cook. She served people in her living room, and, when that became too much, she took over the food operations at Buffalo Bill's, a nearby bar and restaurant.

DON'T MISS: Vientiane Café offers many vegan, vegetarian, and gluten-free dishes.

Top right: Manorack, Daovy, and Sunny Phanthavong.

Above left: Vientiane Café.

Above right: Spicy basil stir fry.

In 2002, the family opened Vientiane Café. It's named after the largest city in Laos, on the banks of the Mekong River near the border of Thailand. The small, family-run BYOB serves homestyle Lao-Thai cuisine. The two cuisines are similar except for the rice, fish sauce, and spices. In Laos, it's traditional to use sticky rice, a fermented fish sauce called padek, and lots of bird's eye chilis, called mak phet. There's no longer a blue tent, but Daovy and her family love sharing their culture and cuisine with the community that still includes many people from Laos and Thailand looking for a taste of home, neighbors, students, and one last biker who is still a regular.

4728 Baltimore Ave., 215-726-1095

vientiane-cafe.com

PORTABELLOS OF KENNETT SQUARE

Where you'll never walk alone

Portabellos of Kennett Square had only been open a week when a customer asked to talk to the owner. Chef Brett Hulbert and his wife, Sandra, were nervous. They knew that word of mouth in such a small town could make or break their new restaurant.

Their fears were realized when the customer, Alan King, told them he would *not* be a regular. To their relief, it wasn't because he was unhappy with his meal. To their dismay, he explained that it was because he was eighty-five years old, fighting cancer, and didn't expect to be around much longer. Then the retired opera singer broke out in a robust rendition of "You'll Never Walk Alone," enchanting the Hulberts and the surprised guests in the crowded restaurant. Teary-eyed, Sandra promised that they would throw him a party on his ninetieth birthday.

King and his wife patronized the restaurant about once a week, and the two couples bonded over dinners, conversations, and holiday meals as he successfully fought cancer. The day of his ninetieth birthday brought a thirty-one-inch snowstorm, but that didn't prevent the Hulberts from hosting the birthday party for King and twenty-five family members who had come from as far away as California and Texas to eat his favorite dishes, including Dover sole and crab cakes.

Kennett Square is just the kind of place where strangers become friends, as the Hulberts could tell from the first time they walked through the small town. Everyone was friendly even before they knew the couple was considering moving there and buying a business. Brett, who cut his teeth at big, glitzy casinos in Atlantic

Left: Portabello's of Kennett Square Chef Brett Hulbert. Photo by Christa Neu.
Right: Mr. King on his 90th birthday.

City, liked the idea of cooking on a more personal scale, and he was betting that Kennett Square was the perfect place.

In 2011, the couple took over management of Portabellos of Kennett Square. Seven years later, they added a liquor license and moved into a bigger space. The New American restaurant uses seafood from the Mid-Atlantic region and local Chester County products, including specialty teas from nearby Mrs. Robinson's Tea Shop, ice cream from La Michoacana Homemade Ice Cream (see page 168), mushrooms from Phillips Mushroom Farms delivered by The Mushroom Cap (see page 168), and dairy products from Woodside Farm Creamery.

For a taste of Kennett Square mushrooms, choose the Exotic Mushroom Crepe or Beef Stroganoff with Cremini mushrooms. For a taste of small-town living, save time to stroll the charming main streets of Kennett Square.

108 E. State St., Kennett Square, PA, 610-925-4984
portabellosofkennettsquare.com

POP'S HOMEMADE ITALIAN ICE

Or "wooder ice" as locals say

It's unclear who invented water ice, a frozen treat that tastes like a mashup between a snow cone and a slushy, but it's widely believed that it arrived in Philadelphia with the wave of Italian immigrants in the late nineteenth and early twentieth centuries. Filippo "Pop" Italiano, who is considered the granddaddy of water ice in Philadelphia, started selling from a pushcart in 1932. One hot summer day, even before Pop could get the cart out of his garage, a line started to form. That's when he realized that he didn't have to keep pushing the heavy cart around his South Philadelphia neighborhood, and he started selling the water ice from his home.

Six of Pop's grandchildren run Pop's today in a newer building at the same location. The traditional flavors—lemon, cherry, chocolate—are still popular among overheated locals, as is the grove-style peach, which is only available when peaches are in season (late June through early September). Vegans love water ice too because it is dairy-free.

The original location is close to Citizens Bank Park, making a post-Phillies game stop a ritual for many fans. There's a second location in Havertown, a Philadelphia suburb. Open from early March through the end of September.

1337 Oregon Ave., 215-551-7677

150 W. Eagle Rd., Havertown, PA, 610-789-7677

popsice.com

Top: Pop's six grandchildren, circa 1987.

Above left: Pop's Homemade Italian Ice. Photo courtesy of Pop's Homemade Italian Ice.

Above center: Filippo "Pop" Italiano, circa 1932.

Above right: Peach water ice. Photo courtesy of Pop's Homemade Italian Ice.

Other popular stops for water ice include:

John's Water Ice (opened in 1945)
701 Christian St.
7315 Park Ave., Pennsauken, NJ
johnswaterice.com

Rita's Water Ice (throughout Philadelphia and more than five hundred locations)
ritasice.com

DON'T MISS: Don't be confused by the local lingo. Philadelphians usually call it water ice, not Italian Ice and with their accent, that sounds like "wooder ice."

MISS RACHEL'S PANTRY

Charming vegan BYOB

Five-year-old Rachel Klein told her mother that she didn't want to eat anything with faces. She stuck with that throughout her childhood, even when it meant learning to make her own dinner. As she grew, so did her conviction, and she eventually decided to become vegan. Now, at Miss Rachel's Pantry, she helps others eat vegan, whether as part of their regular diet or just for a meal. Only about half of her customers are vegan. As she says, "You don't have to be Chinese to eat Chinese food."

Miss Rachel's Pantry is a cozy spot with a communal farmhouse table for twelve and a few smaller tables for two. It serves six-course, prix-fixe dinners, hosts cooking classes and private events, does catering, and makes take-home casseroles. Klein, a self-taught chef, worked in restaurant kitchens throughout the city. She has continued her education by studying techniques for making tofu, seitan, and other vegan staples; visiting farms; and even learning to make her own coconut milk and vegan cheese. She specializes in playful, homemade food that draws on a variety of cultures, including her own interpretations of Italian and Jewish foods. She uses pickling, spices, sauces, and slaws to draw out flavors. She delights in pairing heavy with light and sweet with savory and strives to keep things interesting with unusual pairings.

One such unusual pairing is the charming BYOB nestled between auto repair shops on a small street in South Philadelphia. Like its neighbors, the front of the shop has a garage door which can be lifted to let in a breeze. But, unlike the mechanic shops on the street,

DON'T MISS: The hechsher–Miss Rachel's Pantry is kosher.

Left: Miss Rachel's Pantry exterior.

Right: Vegan cheese plate at Rachel's Pantry. Photo by Dustin Harder *The Vegan Roadie.*

the small cafe has a charming retro decor. Old-school furnishings are complemented by old photos, flowered china, and vintage advertisements that use the word "pantry," most of which Klein collected at flea markets and on eBay.

The name of her cafe was also adopted from yesteryear. In the 1950s, her grandparents had a luncheonette called "The Pantry," just two miles away in what is now Joseph Fox Bookshop. Food and restaurants are clearly in her DNA. While her father, a well-known food writer, originally discouraged her from getting into the food business, he's now her greatest cheerleader and business advisor.

1938 S. Chadwick St., 215-798-0053

missrachelspantry.com

VIETNAM CAFÉ & RESTAURANT

Hardworking family built successful business

In 1978, Nhu Lai, his wife, Thuyen Luu, and their eight children fled Vietnam in a small, cramped boat. After several days adrift without enough food, water, or fuel, they were rescued and taken to a refugee camp in Malaysia. They spent nine months there before boarding a plane to Philadelphia.

The family arrived in Philadelphia with few possessions and no knowledge of English but were determined to rebuild their lives in their new country.

Within five years, they had saved up enough money to open Fu-Wah Mini Market, a market and deli in University City. In 1984, they opened Vietnam Restaurant, a small BYOB on the outskirts of Philadelphia's Chinatown (see page 90). The market and restaurants catered to Vietnamese who missed the cuisine of their homeland and soon attracted the attention of others who wanted to try the authentic dishes.

The children grew up and joined the family business, which expanded. In 1996, Vietnam Restaurant took over a larger location. In 2008, they opened Vietnam Café in University City just a few doors down from Fu-Wah Mini Market.

Signature dishes include their Vermicelli Noodle Bowls and pork, fish, and seafood Claypots. When the restaurant added a liquor license, the Polynesian cocktails really "caught fire," including the outrageous Flaming Volcano, a flaming drink for two made with rum, vodka, gin, brandy, grenadine, Bacardi 151, and fruit juice.

In the years since, the family-run business has grown and prospered. The children, who all grew up working in the family

Top: Brothers Dave Lai, Ley Lai, and Benny Lai (from left) with their mom, Thuyen Luu.

Above left: The two-person Flaming Volcano. Photo by Brett Thomas Photography.

Above right: Vermicelli Noodle Bowl. Photo by Brett Thomas Photography.

business, now run the restaurants and market, though Luu still oversees recipes and menus. Benny, who was in elementary school when his family arrived in America and often served as their interpreter, handles operations, and other siblings work in the kitchen and in management. Vietnam Restaurant and Vietnam Café have both expanded, and in the ultimate nod of approval, Fu-Wah's tofu banh mi (Vietnamese hoagie) was recently named one of the best sandwiches in America by *Food & Wine* magazine.

Vietnam Café, 816 S. 47th St., 215-729-0260

eatatvietnam.com

Vietnam Restaurant, 221 N. 11th St., 215-592-1163

eatatvietnam.com

Fu-Wah Mini Market, 810 S. 47th St., 215-729-2993

fuwahminimarket.com

Steal away for an hour in the pie shop named for the thief bird

Holly Ricciardi, chef/owner of Magpie Artisan Pies, grew up in Central Pennsylvania, where she learned to bake by longingly watching her mother make delicious baked goods from scratch. Ricciardi didn't taste her first store-bought cookie until college.

It wasn't until two decades post college that all the ingredients came together, and she realized that her hobby of baking should be her profession. In 2012, she became Philadelphia's pie pioneer, opening the city's first all-pie shop.

Unlike a bakery, where people would be forced to purchase a whole pie, she envisioned a comfortable, welcoming place, where people could get just a slice of pie. She created a warm, inviting shop that feels like a cooler version of your grandmother's house, with retro light fixtures hanging above a cheerful counter, fresh white wainscoting, tin trim reminiscent of a pie chest, and a collection of frilly aprons hanging from hooks. The logo, which resembles a Pennsylvania Dutch hex sign, is a tribute to her ancestry. Framed photos of her grandfather and great-grandmother adorn the walls, and her great-grandmother's handwritten butterscotch pie recipe, which hangs in the entryway, was the inspiration for Holly's signature pie, Butterscotch Bourbon. It's no wonder she believes that pies make us feel loved, as she's decorated her shop with reminders of people she loves.

DON'T MISS: The Pie Milkshake—any slice of sweet pie blended into a vanilla milkshake.

Left: Magpie. Photo by Michael Spain-Smith.

Right: Holly Ricciardi. Photo by Michael Spain-Smith.

Magpie also serves Caramel Apple Pie and other fruit pies, cream pies, custards, and savory pot pies—such as Chicken Pot Pie and Smoked Gouda Mac & Cheese Pot Pie—and quiches. The pies are spiced up with unexpected ingredients, such as pink peppercorns in the apple pie and cardamom in the blueberry. Ricciardi compares her crust to a nest and her penchant for feathering her nest with unfamiliar ingredients to the habits of the shop's namesake, the magpie. Known as the "thief bird," the magpie steals ribbons, buttons, and things it's attracted to for its nest.

Get a slice of pie or take a whole pie home and pretend you made it yourself. If you really would like to make it yourself, take one of Magpie's well-organized, quick-to-sell-out pie-making classes.

1622 South St., 267-519-2904

iluvmagpie.com

Taking taste buds to new heights

What do you get when you mix an international business consultant from Malaysia with a Philadelphian who runs an indoor rock climbing gym? A husband and wife duo running a unique ethnic BYOB in South Philadelphia.

Ange Branca not only felt unfulfilled in her consulting career but also missed the taste of traditional Malaysian cuisine, which dates back to the fourteenth century, when the country was a spice trading hub. So, Ange and her husband, John, opened a restaurant focusing on the Malaysian dishes she learned to make from her mother and grandmother. Their charming BYOB, Saté Kampar, specializes in skewered meat grilled on coconut shell charcoal—the country's most popular street food—freshly made traditional dishes using ingredients from Malaysian suppliers, and Malaysian coffees and teas.

Start with the sate menu, which includes goat, beef, chicken, tofu and pork. Don't be shy about the goat. It is skillfully marinated and grilled. As half of Malaysians are Muslim, there is a separate grill for Halal meats. For the main course, diners choose a base and then a shareable topping that incorporates many flavors and textures, some unfamiliar to the Western palate. Nasi Lemak Bungkus, with its coconut rice, crispy anchovies, hard-boiled egg, and authentic spices wrapped in a banana leaf, is as flavorful and magical a base as the menu promises. Beef, chicken, fish, and vegetarian toppings are available.

Top right: Saté, the restaurant's signature dish. Photo by Kerry McIntyre.

Above left: John and Ange Branca. Photo by Amy McKeever.

Above right: An array of dishes. Photo by Maria Young.

The casual BYOB opened in 2016 and was quickly nominated for Best New Restaurant Award from the James Beard Foundation. What do you get when you mix an international businesswoman with an expert rock climber? A restaurant that takes taste buds to new heights.

1837 E. Passyunk Ave., 267-324-3860
facebook.com/SateKampar

DON'T MISS: Check out the coffee and teas. Thanks to the masterfully illustrated drink menu and glossary, ordering is even simpler than at your neighborhood coffee house. The menu shows how much coffee, tea, condensed milk, evaporated milk and sugar can be found in each drink. Oh, and that coffee ring on the menu? It's part of the design.

HERSHEL'S EAST SIDE DELI

Carrying on his family's legacy

Perhaps it was his family's history that gave Steven Safern the courage to make a midlife career change. After nearly two decades as an engineer, Safern went back to his roots and opened Hershel's East Side Deli, an authentic Jewish deli in Reading Terminal Market.

In the 1930s, Safern's grandparents and their six daughters and two sons lived in Dynow, a small town in Southeast Poland, where they owned and operated a market and deli. When the German SS marched into town, their oldest son, Hershel, ran home to find only his younger brother (Safern's father), Pincus. Wounded and terrified, Hershel scooped up his younger brother and took cover. They managed to escape the Nazis and made their way to the Russian border, where they were transported to Siberia. The brothers, the only ones in their family and town to survive the Holocaust, were in Siberia for six years until the war was finally over, and they were able to migrate to America.

In 1946, Hershel got a job at Katz's Deli on the Lower East Side of Manhattan, where he used many of the family recipes from Eastern Europe. The hardworking Eastern European loved his work and carried on the family tradition in the kitchen at Katz's Deli for more than forty years.

Meanwhile, Pincus found work in New York factories and eventually moved to Philadelphia. Steven, Pincus's son, grew up in the City of Brotherly Love, attending Julia Reynolds Masterman School and then Central High School and studied to become an engineer. After nineteen years in engineering, he was making a good living but not living good. Despite his Uncle Hershel's warnings about the difficulties of running a restaurant, Safern

Left: Hershel Family, left to right, Pincus and Hershel with their parents, Chuna and Sarah Safern.

Right: A hearty sandwich from Hershel's. Photo by Michael Chaney of Blackwater Promotions.

wanted to carry on his family's legacy.

Since 2006, Safern has worked alongside his wife, Tina, making traditional Jewish food from scratch at Hershel's East Side Deli, serving up piled-high Reubens, corned beef, house-cured pastrami, matzo ball soup, chicken noodle soup, latkes, kugel, and other homemade deli staples that would undoubtedly make his Uncle Hershel proud, especially since the deli is named in his memory.

Reading Terminal Market
51 N.12th St., 215-922-6220
hershelseastsidedeli.com

DON'T MISS: The best time to visit Reading Terminal Market is before 11:00 a.m. or after 4:00 p.m. It can get quite busy at lunchtime, especially when there's a big convention in town. But, no worries, Hershel's is accustomed to dealing with the crowd and the line moves quickly. Bonus: It's one of a few kiosks that has its own seating.

A taste of Israel

Chef Michael Solomonov called his first restaurant "Zahav," meaning "gold" in Hebrew. When you consider the awards the modern Israeli restaurant has accumulated, you might think the road to his success was paved in gold. It wasn't.

Solomonov was born in Israel, grew up in Pittsburgh, and returned to Israel in his late teens. Although his father is Israeli, Solomonov didn't speak Hebrew, so the only job he could find there was in a bakery. That proved to be his "eureka" moment, where he discovered that he had an affinity for baking. He returned to the United States, got a culinary degree, and then settled in Philadelphia, where he worked at some of the city's most prestigious restaurants.

In 2008, he and his business partner, Steven Cook, created CookNSolo Restaurant Partners and opened Zahav, serving modern Israeli food with influences from Eastern Europe, North Africa, and Persia. The 110-seat restaurant garnered praise from *The New York Times*, *Food & Wine*, *Condé Nast Traveler*, *Esquire*, and *Travel + Leisure*. As his fame was rising, however, Solomonov was sinking into drug and alcohol addiction. The catalyst was the death of his younger brother, David, who was killed in 2003, just three days shy of the end of his tour in the Israeli Defense Forces. After Solomonov's wife and Cook staged an intervention, he worked to get clean and eventually even shared the story of what he called his "double life" with *The New York Times*.

Solomonov and Cook, a chef and Wharton-educated investment banker, went on to have their own gold rush. They opened Dizengoff, patterned after the casual hummusiya popular in Israel, and Abe Fisher, inspired by the American Jewish experience, but better than even a Jewish grandma could make if she was even willing to make modern small plates. That was followed by Goldie, a falafel joint with

Top right: Falafel with all the fixings, fries, and a tehina shake at Goldie. Photo by Michael Persico.

Above left: Chef Michael Solomonov. Photo by Michael Persico.

Above right: Salatim at Zahav. Courtesy CookNSolo Restaurants.

fries and addictive tehina shakes. Cook and Solomonov also have a stake in Federal Donuts, which later led to a philanthropic endeavor, Rooster Soup Company (see page 50).

With restaurant spin-offs in New York, Miami, and Nashville, a movie about Israeli cuisine and several James Beard Awards, the future looks golden.

Zahav
237 St. James Pl., 215-625-8800, zahavrestaurant.com

Abe Fisher
1623 Sansom St., 215-867-0088, abefisherphilly.com

Dizengoff
1625 Sansom St., 215-867-8181, dizengoffhummus.com

Goldie
1526 Sansom St., 215-239-0777, goldiefalafel.com

ROOSTER SOUP COMPANY & FEDERAL DONUTS

A philanthropic venture

Diners can satiate their appetites for food and philanthropy at Rooster Soup Company, whose partners include Celeb Chef Michael Solomonov and his business partner Steven Cook of CookNSolo (see page 48). It was financed, in part, by more than 1,500 people who responded to a crowdsourcing campaign and whose names are embedded in artwork in the restaurant.

Rooster Soup Company serves soups, salads, sandwiches, and comfort foods that all taste just a little bit better than you expect they would in an old-fashioned, diner-like atmosphere. Standouts are the smoked matzo ball soup and Yemenite Chicken Pot Pie. The backbone of the cuisine is five hundred pounds of spare chicken parts from CookNSolo's Federal Donuts, which specializes in Korean-style fried chicken seasoned with za'atar, coconut curry, or buttermilk ranch and donuts in unexpected flavors, such as strawberry lavender and blueberry mascarpone.

All profits from Rooster Soup Company go to support vulnerable Philadelphians through Broad Street Ministry's Hospitality Collaborative, which serves three-course meals to people in need. Along with food, the organization provides clothing, medical care, legal services, housing assistance, and a mailing address, enabling them to get an ID, housing, and employment benefits.

DON'T MISS: The cookbooks. *Zahav: The World of Israeli Cuisine,* published in 2015, and *Israeli Soul,* published in 2018. Plus Solomonov's movie, *In Search of Israeli Cuisine.*

Top: Donuts at Federal Donuts. Photo by Michael Persico.

Above: Mushroom barley, beef and vegetable, smoked matzo ball, and roasted cauliflower soup at Rooster Soup Company. Photo by Michael Persico.

Rooster Soup Company

1526 Sansom St., 215-454-6939

roostersoupcompany.com

Federal Donuts

1219 S. 2nd St., 267-687-8258

1632 Sansom St., 215-665-1101

3428 Sansom St., 267-275-8489

701 N. 7th St., 267-928-3893

Citizens Bank Park, 1 Citizens Bank Park Way, Section 140

Whole Foods, 2101 Pennsylvania Ave.

federaldonuts.com

EAT CAFÉ & ROSA'S FRESH PIZZA

Do well by eating well

Diners at EAT Café get to enjoy a freshly made meal while knowing they're helping those struggling with food insecurity and other issues do the same. The pay-what-you-can cafe is a nonprofit venture with hearty meals and a welcoming atmosphere that's a collaboration between Drexel University's Center for Hunger-Free Communities, Drexel's Center for Hospitality and Sports Management, Vetri Community Partnership (see page 146), and the West Philadelphia community.

The cozy restaurant, with colorful walls lined with artwork by local artists, offers a new menu each week. Guests get a three-course meal with three options to choose from for each course for a suggested price of fifteen dollars or a lighter version for a suggested price of five dollars. Guests are asked to pay the suggested amount, more, less, or nothing. No one goes hungry at EAT Café.

Another restaurant helping others is Rosa's Fresh Pizza. When Mason Wartman left Wall Street to open a pizzeria, his life took an unexpected turn. A customer offered to pay it forward, paying for an extra slice for one of the many homeless people the pizzeria served. Wartman marked a sticky note and posted it on the wall, where someone could use it to pay for pizza. Other customers soon followed the lead, and the walls of Rosa's Fresh Pizza were covered in sticky

DON'T MISS: Feel moved by their missions? In addition to patronizing the restaurants, you can make donations on their websites.

Top right: A three-course meal at EAT Café. Photo by EAT Café staff.

Above left: Mason Wartman, owner, Rosa's Fresh Pizza, in front of a wall of sticky notes.

Above right: A server at EAT Café. Photo by EAT Café staff.

notes. When the walls had five hundred of them, Wartman started keeping track at the register instead, and the walls are now covered with notes of encouragement and thanks. Not only has Rosa's become a reliable source of food for homeless people, but it's also a place where people who might not have crossed paths will interact.

EAT Café
3820 Lancaster Ave., 267-292-2768
eatcafe.org

Rosa's Fresh Pizza
25 S. 11th St.
16 S. 40th St.
215-627-6727
rosasfreshpizza.com

Little menu/big heart

Mexican families and tattooed hipsters share bright floral-covered tables in the tiny dining room at El Compadre, located in the heart of the Italian market. They come for the authentic lamb and pork barbacoa that's marinated, steamed overnight wrapped in maguey leaves, and chopped to order with handmade tortillas and help-yourself fixings.

The barbacoa isn't the whole story. After being fired from a restaurant job for being an undocumented worker, Cristina Martinez started cooking early morning meals in her home kitchen for neighborhood night-shift workers getting off work. Those meals grew into a food truck and eventually the full-fledged restaurant South Philly Barbacoa. In 2016, *Bon Appétit* named this modest restaurant one of the best new restaurants in the country, recognizing the talents of Martinez and her husband, Ben Miller. After her son tragically passed away in his early twenties a year later, the couple merged South Philly Barbacoa with his restaurant, El Compadre, keeping the menu of the former and the space and name of the latter.

The entrance to the restaurant is marked by a colorful mosaic mural by local artist Isaiah Zagar, and inside there's a lot more than good, homestyle Mexican cooking. Cristina and Ben use the publicity the restaurant generates as a platform to tell the story behind the food. They are vocal advocates for the rights of undocumented workers in the United States, especially those in the

Left: Ben Miller and Cristina Martinez. Photo by Michael Klein.

Right: El Compadre barbacoa. Photo by Ted Nghiem.

restaurant industry. They host films, dinners, and teach-ins to build community and encourage greater understanding of the plight of undocumented workers, such as Martinez.

1149 S. 9th St., 267-746-7658

facebook.com/calle9ElCompadre

DON'T MISS: The beverages including the housemade agua frescos and freshly squeezed orange juice and café de olla (a traditional Mexican coffee).

Decadent desserts, coffees, and hot chocolates

Practically the last stop in Philadelphia's Italian Market, just before the two cheesesteak joints that anchor the neighborhood, is a French coffee shop called RIM Café. Owner Rene Kobeitri is a colorful character, as one might expect of a Frenchman with the chutzpah to sell coffee in the heart of the Italian community. He started out as a caterer and restaurateur along the French Riviera, dabbled in printing and computers in the late 1980s, and even opened the first cyber café in Nice before immigrating to Philadelphia in 2006. At that point, he left high tech for old school, opening RIM Café. Within a year, the café's hot chocolate was awarded a "best of" from *Philadelphia* magazine. That led to inclusion on many "best hot chocolate" lists and coverage on the Food Network.

Kobeitri's thick French accent, warmth, and vigorous laugh make him nearly as irresistible as his drinks, which he insists are one-of-a-kind, "no bullsh*t." Whether it's sweet potato coffee using a tuber the size of a football or the signature hot chocolate, which is called a Chocolate Volcano, patrons are in for a show involving rivers of chocolate, streams of caramel sauce, and quite possibly singing and bongo playing.

Kobeitri places a clear glass mug on a chocolate-covered turntable, adds a dollop of whipped cream, and then thick, rich hot cocoa. As the turntable spins, he grates chocolate in flavors ranging from pistachio to parmesan into the decadent dessert. The ribbons of

> **DON'T MISS:** Caffeine addict? RIM Café is attempting to set a record for serving the world's strongest espresso, and its syphon coffee is a standout too.

Rene Kobeitri, owner, RIM Café.

chocolate are topped with gooey, oozy waterfalls of sauce that drip down the inside and outside of the mug. Ask for the crème brûlée volcano and he'll top your drink with marshmallows and then roast them with a blow torch. Sip, spoon, and swallow the seductive concoction in the animal-print booth surrounded by overlapping layers of memorabilia and you'll know you have stumbled across someplace special.

1172 S. 9th St., 215-465-3515

rimcafe.com

A feast for the eyes and the belly

Suraya, the Lebanese all-day cafe and market in Fishtown, is a feast for the eyes as well as the belly—the reds, yellows, and greens of the Lebanese cuisine, the hand-painted mugs, and the bright sunny space. It's enough to motivate a Luddite to create an Instagram account and inspire those already addicted to Instagram to pick up their phones before their forks. But definitely pick up your fork because the man'oushe (Lebanese flatbread), salads, hummous, teas, and pastries taste as good as they look.

The twelve-thousand-square-foot all-day cafe has 125 seats, including a twenty-seat dining counter surrounding an open kitchen with a charcoal grill and wood stone oven; a four-thousand-square-foot outdoor seating area and bar with a fire pit; and a Middle Eastern pantry. The design of the restaurant is inspired by the neighborhood where Nathalie Richan and her brother, Roland Kassis, grew up in Beirut, Lebanon. The siblings named the restaurant for their grandmother, Suraya Harouni, who raised them and kept their family together during tumultuous war-torn times. Suraya was reportedly passionate about not only her family but also good food, which she willingly shared with anyone in need.

Richan and Kassis, joined by Nick Kennedy and Greg Root of ROOT restaurant + wine bar, created this Middle Eastern oasis, which is open from early morning until late at night moving from breakfast pastries to Arak and cocktails with names adapted from the poetry of Khalil Gibran.

The shelves of the cafe are like a modern-day bazaar where diners can purchase the colorfully painted mugs and bowls used at the restaurant as well as imported spices, olive oils, cookbooks, sweets, and fresh salads and dips to go.

Top: Mezze Plate. Photo by Melissa Alam.

Above left: Suraya interior. Photo by Melissa Alam.

Above right: Suraya Baba Ganoush. Photo by Melissa Alam.

In Lebanon, they say, "Ahlan Wa Sahlan, Sahtein," which loosely translates to "Welcome, enjoy your meal" and embodies the spirit of the cafe and its namesake, Suraya Harouni.

1528 Frankford Ave., 215-302-1900

surayaphilly.com

Cheese heaven

Brothers Danny and Joe Di Bruno emigrated from Italy in the 1930s expecting to find streets paved in gold. Instead, they found the cobblestone streets of Philadelphia's Italian Market (9th Street from Wharton to Fitzwater) in South Philadelphia. The brothers, who had only a third-grade education but were highly motivated, opened a grocery store that soon evolved into a cheese shop. The tiny seven-hundred-square-foot store is packed with thousands of pounds of imported cheese and cured meats hanging from the ceiling, wooden barrels of olives, shelves of olive oils, and gourmet foods.

Their grandsons, Emilio, Bill, and Bill Jr., took over in 1990 and added four more locations and an online store. The Rittenhouse Square, Washington Square, Comcast Center, and Ardmore Farmers Market locations have the same amazing selection in updated atmospheres. The ten-thousand-square-foot Rittenhouse Square store has produce, meat, and fish counters as well as prepared foods, charcuterie, a cafe, and a large cheese area. Well-trained cheesemongers are happy to help guests create the perfect cheese plate with pairings (and they are generous with samples too!). The forty-five-hundred-square-foot Washington Square location has wine and craft beer on tap and bottled, plus more than three hundred cheeses from around the world.

For an immersive experience, book DiBruno After Hours. The two-hour private tasting and shopping event can be booked at the original location in South Philadelphia or in the Washington Square store. During the BYOB-friendly event, guests sample composed plates of cheese paired with fruits, nuts, jellies, and other goodies plus practically anything else in the shop.

The grandsons have done their family legacy proud. In 2006, Di Bruno Bros. was named Gourmet Retailer of the Year by the

Top: Left to right, Bill, Jr., Bill, and Emilio Mignucci. Photo courtesy of Di Bruno Bros.

Above left: Di Bruno cheese. Photo courtesy of Di Bruno Bros.

Above right: Rittenhouse location. Photo courtesy of Di Bruno Bros.

Specialty Food Association, and in 2013 they worked with Tenaya Darlington, known as "Madame Fromage" to publish *Di Bruno Bros. House Of Cheese: A Guide To Wedges, Recipes & Pairings.*

930 S. 9th St., the original location, 215-922-2876

1730 Chestnut St., 215-665-9220

Comcast Center, 1701 JFK Blvd., 215-531-5666

834 Chestnut St., 267-519-3115

120 Coulter Ave., Ardmore, PA, 484-416-3311

dibruno.com

More than a cooking class—dinner and a show

At COOK, top chefs conduct demonstration-style cooking classes in a state-of-the-art kitchen surrounded by a sixteen-seat counter. It's not an ordinary cooking class. It's like live dinner theater. The intimate space allows participants to connect with the chefs—asking questions, picking up tips and watching them cook. At evening classes participants get a full meal including wine. During daytime classes, participants may get either a full meal or snacks and tastings. It's a fun, interactive experience that will delight even those foodies who aren't typically interested in cooking classes. It's a treat for chefs too, as they usually cook for people they don't see and rarely get to watch guests enjoying their food.

About twenty-five classes are offered each month, including classes with chefs, cookbook authors, and mixologists as well as classes focusing on knife skills, butchering, and even competitions.

COOK is the brainchild of restaurateur Audrey Claire, who opened it in 2011 to support the local food community.

253 S. 20th St., 215-735-2665
audreyclairecook.com

DON'T MISS: COOK's monthly e-newsletter with its list of classes. To get one of the coveted sixteen seats, sign up for a class as soon as the list arrives in your inbox.

Top: Chef Michael Solomonov. Photo by Yoni Nimrod.

Above left: Chef Terence Feury. Photo by Michael Spain-Smith.

Above right: Dining at COOK. Photo by Yoni Nimrod.

From buddies to business partners

Brian Sirhal and Tim Spinner met at West Windsor-Plainsboro High School near Princeton. Spinner, then a long-haired surfer type called "Spin," hung out with Sirhal's twin brother, Geoff. The twins (Brian and Geoff) had separate but overlapping groups of friends who often hung out together. Sirhal recalls that during their senior year of high school Geoff was once grounded for a month when "Spin" failed to corroborate a fictitious story covering up some high school mischief.

Despite that mishap, the friendship between Brian and Tim deepened during college when they both had summer jobs at PGA golf tournaments, where they worked hard and played hard.

After college, Spinner determined that corporate life wasn't for him, and he rerouted to The Restaurant School at Walnut Hill College. He worked alongside Chef Jose Garces (see page 198) at Stephen Starr's El Vez (see page 200) and then worked for Garces at Amada and Distrito, where Spinner helped garner mentions on *Esquire*'s list of "Top 20 New Restaurants in the U.S." and *Condé Nast Traveler*'s "Top 50 Tables in the World." When Sirhal became disenchanted with his finance career on Wall Street, he joined Spinner at Distrito, learning front of the house and bar operations.

In 2011, the two Garces proteges struck out on their own with Cantina Feliz, a contemporary Mexican restaurant in Fort Washington, which was followed a year later by La Calaca Feliz in Fairmount and then Taqueria Feliz in Manayunk. All of the restaurants have bright, fanciful decor featuring Day of the Dead murals by local artist Allison Dilworth. They've become known for their creative, yet traditional Mexican cuisine and tequila-focused bars with beloved tequila flights.

After hours Sirhal and Spinner can still be found hanging out

Left: La Calaca Feliz. Photo by Courtney Apple Photography.

Right: Chef Tim Spinner (left) and Brian Sirhal. Photo by Jason Varney.

together, now with their wives and children too. After all these years, they no longer call each other by their last names, but they still call each other's parents "Mr. and Mrs." After twenty-five years, they seem to communicate with a secret language that amuses their coworkers but keeps each of their restaurants running like a well-oiled machine.

Cantina Feliz

424 S. Bethlehem Pike, Fort Washington, PA, 215-646-1320

felizrestaurants.com

La Calaca Feliz

2321 Fairmount Ave., 215-787-9930

Taqueria Feliz

4410 Main St., Manayunk, PA, 267-331-5874

History repeating itself for the Mink family

In 1947, Samuel Mink purchased a restaurant called Kelly's, a Philadelphia institution attracting those in the legal industry and politicos from nearby City Hall. The former lawyer ran the restaurant until his sudden death in 1969. His son, David, who was born the year Mink purchased the restaurant and was by then twenty-two years old, dropped out of his Ivy League college and took over the family business. A year later he opted out and it was sold.

By 1976, David regretted his decision and opened an oyster house a few blocks south at the site of the current Oyster House on Sansom Street. He had a son the same year and named him Sam after his father. Eventually, David was ready to sell the restaurant and hoped to pass it down to his son, but Sam, by then twenty-four years old and fresh out of college, opted out and it was sold.

A few years later history repeated itself. In 2008, Sam changed his mind and bought the failing restaurant back from its owners. The third generation restaurateur added a raw bar serving an extensive selection of oysters on the half shell, focusing on local varieties from the Mid-Atlantic up to New England and Canada. He renovated and modernized the menu and restaurant, hanging his collection of more than one hundred vintage oyster plates.

Over the tides of time, the Mink family repeated its history and once again owns a seafood restaurant that is a Philadelphia institution.

1516 Sansom St., 215-567-7683
oysterhousephilly.com

Top left: David and Sam Mink. Photo by Jason Varney.

Top right: Oyster House Table. Photo by Jason Varney.

Above left: Interior. Photo by Jason Varney.

Above right: Restaurant Week at Oyster House. Photo by Steve Legato. Courtesy of Center City District.

DON'T MISS: The street sign from Mole Street, home of the Mink family's original restaurant, above the bar.

What's in a name?

A three-year-old is responsible for Hungry Pigeon's quirky but fitting name. Whenever the landlord's daughter saw 743 S. Fourth Street, it was surrounded by pigeons, so the observant preschooler dubbed it "the pigeon building." Chefs Scott Schroeder and Pat O'Malley could have been irritated about the birds but decided to embrace them instead by calling their restaurant the Hungry Pigeon.

The theme is carried out throughout the all-day café, where there's a communal farm table topped with a large light fixture made of bird cages and surrounded by artwork of pigeons by local artists. Schroeder's then-girlfriend-now-wife, an artist, designed the bibbed pigeon logo and decorated the restaurant along with O'Malley's then-girlfriend-now-wife. Pigeons (called squab) are often on the menu at the homey spot.

The restaurant serves creative American comfort food that's shareable and includes many vegetarian and vegan options. More than 95 percent of the food is from small producers, including the chicken, duck, pheasant, game hens, and the succulent baby turkey, which is raised outdoors by a small farmer in Glen Rock, Pennsylvania. Schroeder, an overall-wearing chef who trained with Chef Georges Perrier, Stephen Starr (see page 200), and others, handles savory foods. His partner, O'Malley, who has a degree in

DON'T MISS: The restaurant. Its name isn't on the sign; there's just a drawing of a bib-wearing pigeon. Or look for the mural that says "Serving Lunch Breakfast Dinner" painted along the outside wall of the restaurant.

Hungry Pigeon exterior. Photo by Neal Santos.

Culinary Arts from the Art Institute of Philadelphia and was pastry chef at New York City's Balthazar for eight years, is responsible for sweet foods, breads, and pastry. They met when working together at Guillermo Pernot's now-closed restaurant ¡Pasión!

The restaurant has a relaxed vibe with exposed brick walls, wooden tables, and vintage storefront windows. In addition to the regular tables, there's a counter as well as the farm table, which can also be used as a communal table or a semi-private dining room for fourteen diners. Despite the name, there is nothing fly-by-night at this neighborhood restaurant. After earning outstanding reviews from the local restaurant critics, it's clearly here to stay.

743 S. 4th St., 215-278-2736
hungrypigeon.com

Philadelphia classic reinvented

When Fork opened in 1997, Le Bec Fin, Bookbinders, and Striped Bass were some of the city's most popular restaurants. They're all gone now, but Fork's future looks bright.

Over the years, Fork has weathered not only competition but also shifts in diners' expectations. Since its early days, Food Network, social media, online review sites, and even websites have all become part of the food landscape.

The secret to Fork's survival might be the vision of owner Ellen Yin who believes that a restaurant must reinvent itself on an ongoing basis.

Perhaps Yin's path to becoming a restaurateur forecasts her adaptability. After earning degrees from the University of Pennsylvania and trying other career paths, Yin's experiences working in restaurants in her teens became a siren's song luring her back.

She worked with designer Marguerite Rodgers on the decor, which is smart and elegant, with a warm glow, like Yin herself. Over the years, the look has evolved. Tablecloths disappeared when they started to feel formal and stuffy, and a mural by artist and longtime server Anthony DeMelas was added.

The contemporary American food changed too. Yin let the chefs—Anne-Marie Lasher, Dave Ballentine, Thien Ngo, Terence Feury, and Eli Kulp—express their creativity. Fork was one of the first restaurants in the area to focus on seasonality and local farmers and artisans before it was the trendy thing to do.

In 2014, Yin and Kulp, now a co-owner, opened High Street on Market next door and soon after took over the reins at a.kitchen+bar.

National accolades started rolling in. High Street on Market was named second-best new restaurant in the U.S. by *Bon Appétit*,

Left: Charcuterie at a.kitchen. Photo by Chaucee Stillman.

Right: Ellen Yin at Fork. Photo by Catherine Karnow.

and one of the best new restaurants in the world by *Travel & Leisure*. Kulp was named to *Food & Wine*'s list of Best New Chefs, and a.kitchen+bar made *Wine Enthusiast*'s list of Top 100 wine restaurants in the country.

Building on the momentum, Yin and Kulp then started planning the opening of High Street on Hudson in New York City. The script had to be rewritten on May 12, 2015, when Kulp was paralyzed in an Amtrak train derailment. But the show went on, and High Street on Hudson opened later that year. Kulp, known for his sophisticated palate, continues to work closely with the chefs at all the restaurants on leadership and menu development, including Executive Chef John Patterson at Fork.

The restaurants continued to draw national attention. In 2016, Kulp was a James Beard Foundation Finalist for Best Chef, Mid-Atlantic. That same year High Street on Hudson in New York City was named one of *Food & Wine*'s Best New Restaurants of the Year, and in 2017 it made Michelin's Bib Gourmand list. For more than twenty years, Fork has managed to stay on top of its game.

Fork, 306 Market St., 215-625-9425, forkrestaurant.com

High Street on Market, 308 Market St., 215-625-0988, highstreetonmarket.com

a.kitchen+a.bar, 135 S. 18th St., 215-825-7030, akitchenandbar.com

From elephant to elegant

Greg Vernick's culinary experiences grew from elephant to elegant. In high school, he washed dishes and scooped water ice at Lucy the Elephant, a beloved landmark at the Jersey Shore. After graduating from Boston University and the Culinary Institute of America, Vernick trained with some of the country's most celebrated chefs, including Jean-Georges Vongerichten, and worked on openings of Vongerichten's new restaurants in Boston; Park City, Utah; Vancouver; Tokyo; and Qatar.

Fortunately, he traveled home to Philadelphia to open his namesake restaurant, Vernick Food & Drink. He grew up in Cherry Hill, New Jersey, a suburb of Philadelphia. His grandparents lived in a carriage house behind his family's home, and his mother owned a restaurant nearby. Vernick loved spending time in the restaurant kitchen with his grandfather, a tough man with a soft spot for his grandson. Vernick recalls mixing together random, mismatched ingredients from the restaurant pantry that his grandfather would willingly taste.

Vernick's grandfather previously owned a butcher shop at 21st and Rodman in the Rittenhouse Square neighborhood, just a few blocks from where Vernick opened his eponymous restaurant in 2012. Vernick had come full circle—returning to the neighborhood where his grandfather spent much of his career and becoming the third generation of his family to enter the food business.

His restaurant, housed in a nineteenth century brownstone, sports large windows, a vibrant bar, and a popular chef's counter. When it opened, *Bon Appétit* dubbed it one of the best new restaurants in America. Accolades followed from *Food & Wine*, *The New York Times*, *The Washington Post*, and *USA Today*, and in 2017, Vernick was

Left: Chef Greg Vernick. Photo by Steve Legato.

Right: Vernick. Photo by Rebekah Lynn Photography.

named James Beard's Best Chef, Mid-Atlantic.

Vernick describes his style as simple, seasonal, and approachable and notes that simple isn't easy because there's nowhere to hide. He uses high-quality ingredients, coaxing big flavors from his wood-fired grill. He is known for his carefully curated toasts, each delicately balanced so that the flavor of the bread doesn't overwhelm the toppings.

Vernick now spends time in the kitchen mixing ingredients into simple but sophisticated dishes under the watchful eye of his grandfather, whose photo hangs near the restaurant kitchen.

2031 Walnut St., 267-639-6644

vernickphilly.com

DON'T MISS: Vernick Seafood and a new restaurant by Jean-Georges Vongerichten opening in the Four Seasons Philadelphia in the Comcast Technology Tower in Fall 2018.

Gritty streets with great restaurants

When you walk the main drags of Fishtown, you can pretty much count on seeing new construction around every corner, public art on the sides of buildings and on the arms and legs of the millennials who live there, as well as trendy restaurants and bars serving up dishes you will soon find in your Instagram newsfeed. This quickly gentrifying area is attracting creative types and hipsters due to its affordability, proximity to Center City Philadelphia, and its undeniable coolness. The frequent trains zooming by on the raised tracks of the elevated subway, called the El, set the soundtrack for the neighborhood and create shadowy, bridge-covered streets.

The formerly working-class area named after its history in shad fishing is full of modest row houses and independent businesses, and is home to some of Philadelphia's trendiest restaurants, including Wm. Mulherin's Sons (see page 164); Cheu Fishtown (see page 78); Suraya, a Levant-inspired restaurant (see page 58); and Kensington Quarters, a meat-centric restaurant with surprisingly good vegetable dishes. Kensington Quarters has a large outside dining area, as do many of the eateries along Frankford Avenue, and offers regular classes, including whole animal butchery. Its neighbors include Stephen Starr's Fette Sau and Frankford Hall (see page 200) and charming Good Spoon, whose flavorful soups can also be found at farmers markets throughout the region. Nearby are Front Street Cafe (see page 20), with its freshly squeezed juice bar, inviting patio, and farm-to-table organic food, including many vegetarian options; Pizza Brain (see page 94); Little Baby's Ice Cream (see pages 94); and an industrial chic location of La Colombe Coffee Roasters (see page 142). The neighborhood is also home to several other distilleries and breweries, including Philadelphia Distilling (see page 158), Rowhouse Spirits, and Evil Genius.

Top: Fishtown. Photo courtesy of Good Spoon.

Above: Kensington Quarters. Photo by Jen Bragan.

Kensington Quarters, 1310 Frankford Ave., 267-314-5086, kensingtonquarters.com

Good Soup, 1400 N. Front St., 267-239-5787, goodspoonfoods.com

Philadelphia Distilling, 25 E. Allen St., 215-671-0346, philadelphiadistilling.com

Rowhouse Spirits, 2440 Frankford Ave., 267-825-7332, rowhousespirits.us

Evil Genius, 1727 N. Front St., 215-425-6820, evilgeniusbeer.com

Front Street Cafe, 1253 N. Front St., 215-5515-3073, frontstreetcafe.net

> **DON'T MISS:** Joe Beddia, whose pizza was dubbed "Best in America" by *Bon Appétit*, is opening an expanded pizzeria in Fishtown. The cult favorite is sure to be an instant hit.

METROPOLITAN BAKERY

In the sweet spot between business success and social responsibility

Twenty-five years ago most Americans were eating soft, flavorless white bread. Wendy Smith Born and James Barrett, who met at White Dog Cafe, a progressive West Philly cafe where Born was a managing partner and Barrett was pastry chef, bonded over their love of France, especially the chewy breads. The duo took a chance that the naturally leavened, hand-shaped breads might catch on here, too, and, with some trepidation, decided to open their first Metropolitan Bakery. It became clear about a week before their official opening date that their idea was destined to be successful.

The Philadelphia Inquirer wrote an article praising Metropolitan's crusty, flavorful breads listing an opening date that was a week earlier than the duo had planned. It was 1993, when print reigned and no frantic last-minute tweets could correct the error and let people know that the bakery was still under construction. Born and Barrett did the only thing they could do: they opened anyway. Dodging construction workers and using a shoebox for a register, they sold their first loaves to the growing line of people.

The days that followed were chaotic, with Barrett sleeping in the bakery on sacks of flour and Born delivering loaves at 4:00 a.m., but their hard work paid off. Metropolitan Bakery has become a Philadelphia icon, with three retail outlets, a wholesale business that supplies the city's top restaurants, a thriving online business, and a sit-down cafe BYOB, Metropolitan Cafe & Pizza. They also run a

> **DON'T MISS:** The all-natural granola that was named "best in the U.S." by epicurious.com

Left: Metropolitan breads.

Right: Co-owners James Barrett and Wendy Smith Born. Photo by Kyle Born.

nonprofit gallery, Metropolitan Gallery 250, that supports emerging artists, many of whom work in the city's food industry. Their product line has expanded to include pastries, snacks, and granola.

The bakery has been featured in *O, the Oprah magazine, Saveur, Gourmet, Martha Stewart Living, The Washington Post,* and on NBC's *Today Show.*

Along the way, the duo has sought the sweet spot between business success and social responsibility. The bakery uses and sells locally sourced and sustainable products from area farmers and small producers; partners with local nonprofits, such as Broad Street Ministry and Project HOME; and is committed to providing employment and job training for marginally employable Philadelphians.

262 S. 19th St., original location, 215-545-6655
Reading Terminal Market, 51 N. 12th St., 215-829-9020
4013 Walnut St., 215-222-1492
Metropolitan Cafe & Pizza, 264 S. 19th St., 267-990-8055
metropolitanbakery.com

Admittedly inauthentic

When high school buddies Ben Puchowitz and Shawn Darragh decided to open an Asian-inspired restaurant, they didn't backpack through China sampling Asian delicacies, rifle through food markets searching for spices unfamiliar to Western palates, or meander through food stalls at Beijing's Night Market. Their three hip fusion restaurants aren't authentic, but that's not what they're striving to be. Puchowitz and Darragh aren't trying to re-create the foods found in East Asia or even Chinatown, but instead they decided to serve the kind of food that they like to eat. Judging from the success of their restaurants and the big crowds, it's clearly the food lots of others like to eat too.

The duo opened Cheu Noodle Bar, their interpretation of a "Japanese" Ramen Bar in Washington Square West in 2013. The small, bustling noodle shop was followed by Bing Bing Dim Sum, a riff on a Chinese dim sum parlor, in South Philadelphia and then Cheu Fishtown in Fishtown. They chose to open in neighborhoods chock-full of other young restaurant industry folk looking for adventurous, filling, inexpensive food. Fun bars and cool graffiti-inspired artwork, such as the hipster Dumplings characters on the walls of Bing Bing Dim Sum, didn't hurt either.

Darragh handles the business side, while Puchowitz, who worked in the kitchen at Matyson, a well-liked but now-closed BYOB, handles everything culinary. His cuisine combines his love of Asian food with the flavors of his Jewish childhood. Cheu Fishtown might be the only place in the world where diners can satisfy their hunger with Soybean Falafel or Bubbie Chow's Sliced Beef, featuring char siu brisket. The nontraditional pairing of flavors and

Top left: Ben Puchowitz and Shawn Darragh. Photo by Danya Henninger, Imagic Digital.

Top right: Miso Ramen with pork belly, Brisket Ramen with matzo ball & kimchi, and Coconut Curry Ramen with peanut sambal at Cheu. Photo by Danya Henninger, Imagic Digital.

Above: Cheu Fishtown Interior. Photo by Danya Henninger, Imagic Digital.

styles has become a trademark of the three restaurants. If you're looking for authentic Asian dishes at the hip spots owned by these longtime friends, you've missed the point.

Cheu Noodle, 255 S. 10th St., 267-639-4136, cheunoodlebar.com

Bing Bing Dim Sum, 1648 E. Passyunk Ave., 215-279-7702, bingbingdimsum.com

Cheu Fishtown, 1416 Frankford Ave., 267-758-2269, cheufishtown.com

TERMINI BROS. BAKERY

Two brothers. One dream. Three generations.

Gaetano Termini came to the United States, got a job, and saved money to bring his brother, Giuseppe, from Enna, Sicily. Giuseppe arrived in 1920 with a suitcase, a recipe book, and experience apprenticing as a master baker. Within a year, the brothers had saved enough money from their jobs at the Stetson Hat Company to open a small bakery. It became the "go-to" place for wedding cakes, enabling them to purchase a delivery truck. In 1938, the brothers moved the bakery across the street to a larger space that houses their flagship store today. Giuseppe, his wife, Mariangela, and their newborn son, Vincent, and Gaetano all lived above the store.

During World War II, Termini Brothers Bakery shipped fruitcakes overseas to soldiers on the frontline further enhancing its reputation. By 1954 it needed to expand again in both square footage and personnel. It annexed the buildings behind it to create more space, and Vincent joined the family business.

Giuseppe passed the bakery on to Vincent twenty years later but continued to work there until his death at the age of ninety-five. Vincent's sons, Joey and Vinny, have fond memories of standing on milk crates watching their grandfather fill cannolis. They shared their father's and grandfather's commitment to Termini Bros. and prepared to enter the family business by earning degrees in food marketing from Saint Joseph's University and the Culinary Institute of America, respectively. In 1991, they joined their father and grandfather at the bakery. They initiated a mail order business, introduced new ideas, and opened more locations, but they never changed the recipes their grandfather brought from the old country.

> **DON'T MISS:** The accordion player at the South Philadelphia store on Saturdays.

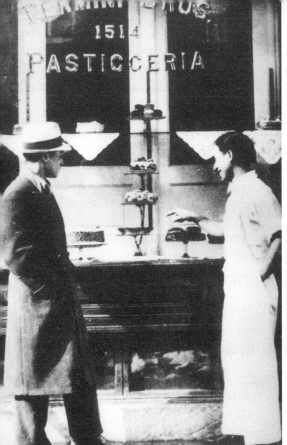

Top right: Cannoli shells.

Above left: The brothers in front of the original bakery.

Above right: Gaetano and Giuseppe inside their bakery, circa 1921.

Today, Termini Brothers Bakery is still known for its cannoli, cream cake, and Italian sweets. As the bakery has been handed down from generation to generation, the family is still using the same recipe that their grandfather brought from Italy and has been instilling the same work ethic in the fourth generation.

1523 S. 8th St., 215-334-1816
1538 Packer Ave., 215-336-1001
Reading Terminal Market, 51 N. 12th St., 215-629-1790
Comcast Center Food Court, 1701 John F. Kennedy Blvd., 215-575-0504
termini.com

Finding killer cocktails

During Prohibition you needed a secret password to get into a speakeasy. Once inside, nearly undrinkable and sometimes even fatal homemade alcohol was served. Bartenders disguised the nasty-flavored moonshine with soda, sugar, herbs, lemon, and fruit juices, creating the nation's first cocktails.

You don't need a password to get into Philadelphia's modern speakeasies, just the 411 on where to find the unmarked entrances. These hard-to-find bars possess a certain *je ne sais quoi*, and you'll drink killer cocktails rather than cocktails that kill.

Franklin Mortgage and Investment Company was named for the country's largest alcohol ring during Prohibition, and behind the plain black door is a dark space reminiscent of a 1920s speakeasy. Franklin Mortgage made *GQ*'s list of Top 25 Cocktail Bars in America and *Bon Appétit*'s list of Top 10 Best New Cocktail Bars. There's no vodka, but there is a long list of innovative and classic cocktails with unusual names that won't disappoint.

One Tippling Place was named to *Food & Wine*'s list of twenty-four best cocktail bars in America. Owner Anne Frey, a former actress, real estate agent, and antique jewelry dealer, envisioned a quiet place for boomers to drink in a 1920s building gently set back from the sidewalk. She created a space that looks like your grandmother's living room if it were decorated by your grandfather's mistress. It's full of tufted sofas and big cushiony chairs stripped of their plastic seat covers and spiced up with quirky artwork and heavy drapes.

DON'T MISS: Hop Sing Laundromat (see page 26), the mother of all speakeasies.

The Grille Room at the Mask & Wig. Photo by Megan Hurry.

Nearby is Ranstead Room, a dark, sexy bar with black leather booths and noteworthy cocktails. Enter from Ranstead, a dark back alley, where there's a black door marked with the logo—two back-to-back Rs—or through El Rey, a Mexican spot where diners are led on a long and winding trip through the restaurant kitchen.

The Mask and Wig Club, the University of Pennsylvania's all-male musical comedy troupe, makes its home in a hard-to-find building that was formerly a stable, church, carriage house, and dissecting rooms for Jefferson Medical College. Nestled in the building is The Grille Room, a rathskeller. Its wood-paneled walls are lined with beer steins and caricatures of members, including thirty-five by Maxfield Parrish. The only way to get access to the bar is by going to one of the clever shows in the upstairs theater.

Franklin Mortgage and Investment Company
112 S. 18th St., 267-467-3277
thefranklinbar.com

1 Tippling Place
2006 Chestnut St., 215-665-0456
1tpl.com

Ranstead Room
2013 Ranstead St., 215-563-3330

The Grille Room in the Mask and Wig Club
310 S. Quince St., 215-716-7378
maskandwig.com

Happily divorced

Michael McNally and Terry Berch McNally have been business partners since 1991, when the chef and the former server took over London Restaurant. While their restaurant has stood the test of time, their marriage hasn't. The couple married in 1988 and divorced in 1996 but still work together every day running their restaurant. He's the chef, and she's the general manager. Although they're no longer a couple, the McNallys are mindful of how their business and their children make them life partners, and to keep lines of communication open, they had a business therapist who made sure that they and their managers all stayed on the same page.

Michael and Terry met when they both worked at 20th Street Cafe (now the site of Twenty Manning). Terry was a server, and Michael was the chef. She fell for his butchering skills and got herself a job in the kitchen to be closer to him. They worked together at several other local restaurants before ending up at London Restaurant in Fairmount. One day in 1991 Michael walked into the owner's office to ask for a raise and walked out with an opportunity to purchase the nearly bankrupt restaurant. He and Terry made an overnight decision to buy it, changing the name to London Grill. They upgraded the draft beer system, created an ambitious craft beer program, and pushed the city to approve outside dining. Then they worked to get the Fairmount neighborhood noticed. Terry's

DON'T MISS: Don't want to cook on Passover, Father's Day, Rosh Hashanah, Thanksgiving, Chanukah, or Christmas Eve? London Grill can always be counted on for holiday meals.

Top left: London interior.

Above left: Terry Berch McNally and Michael McNally.

Above right: London exterior.

biggest feat was getting Fairmount on a map literally—the previous tourist map stopped a few blocks short of Fairmount Avenue—and figuratively—coordinating with nearby restaurants, the closest hotel, and the Eastern State Penitentiary, a prison turned attraction, to bring more tourists to the area.

Two years later they expanded into the building next door, creating Paris Wine Bar, a French-inspired *boîte* serving local sustainable wines and hosting jazz music several nights a week. Over the years, London Grill has become a neighborhood icon with a bar, great list of craft beers, and new American cuisine.

2301-2302 Fairmount Ave., 215-978-4545
londongrill.com

Toughest table in America

To get reservations for the farmhouse table at Talula's Table, a charming country chic eatery in historic Kennett Square, diners must call one year in advance to the day, at 7:00 a.m. Diners must book the entire table, which seats eight to twelve people. Why the hoopla? Because Aimee Olexy, who is also the mastermind behind Talula's Garden, Talula's Daily, and The Love in Center City Philadelphia, designs meals that create lifelong memories for guests.

Condé Nast Traveler calls it "The world's toughest restaurant reservation," and Talula's made the *Saveur* 100 list, the magazine's annual ranking of the most inspiring people, places, gadgets, tastes, and techniques in the food world. *The New York Times* praised the "handsome, deceptively complex and masterfully executed" food, calling the experience a "spiritual retreat."

It's the perfect special occasion venue. It's charming, it's personal, and it's eight courses of nirvana sandwiched between bite-sized appetizers, an irresistible bread basket, and two post-dessert desserts that aren't even counted as part of the eight courses. Each course is beautifully presented, painstakingly prepared, and downright delicious.

The restaurant is a BYOB and provides recommended wine pairings. Or diners can use the occasion to uncork special bottles from their own collection.

DON'T MISS: The chance to snag an earlier reservation by calling and asking about upcoming cancellations. Last-minute openings are also posted in the restaurant's e-newsletter, on its social media pages, and on its website.

Left: Farmhouse Table. Photo by Jaeson Han.

Right: Cheeseplate. Photo by Jaeson Han.

For an insider's view, opt for the secret kitchen table, which seats four to eight people in the kitchen's nerve center under a chandelier made of kitchen utensils. You can chat with the chef and staff, watch dinner being prepared and plated, and enjoy the same exquisitely prepared menu as diners seated in the quaint dining room. It has the intimacy of sitting at your best friend's kitchen counter sharing secrets and sipping wine while dinner is being prepared. The kitchen table can be snagged with "just" a few months' notice.

During the day, Talula's operates as a country market featuring prepared gourmet foods, baked goods, and imported goods to eat in or take out.

102 W. State St., Kennett Square, PA, 610-444-8255

talulastable.com

Stayed close to their roots

Brothers Robert and Benjamin Bynum, Jr., have been an integral part of Philadelphia's restaurant community for more than twenty years. Their family has been a cornerstone of the area's jazz community for even longer.

In the 1950s, the brothers' parents, Ruth and Benjamin Bynum, Sr., were the proprietors of Cadillac Lounge, a jazz venue in North Philadelphia that attracted some of the best artists of the day. Lou Rawls, Gladys Knight and the Pips, and Aretha Franklin all performed at the club, and Billy Pauls even named his first album *Feelin' Good at the Cadillac Club*. In 1977, they turned the venue into Impulse Discotheque, the city's first black-owned disco. It became one of the hottest night clubs of its time, catering to an older, upscale crowd.

The brothers worked there, along with Robert's best buddy, Michael Nutter. Robert met Nutter at Central High School, and they were roommates at the University of Pennsylvania. Among the distinguished guests who frequented Impulse were city council members who inspired Nutter to enter public life and eventually become mayor of Philadelphia.

In 1990, the Bynum brothers opened Zanzibar Blue, a jazz club, on South 11th Street. It moved to a larger space beneath Bellevue Hotel Philadelphia before closing in 2007. Based on the success of Zanzibar Blue, Robert and Benjamin, Jr. went on to open several successful dining and jazz venues. In 1995, they headed for the Delaware River waterfront, where they opened Warmdaddy's, a great jazz venue serving Southern food, followed by Relish, another jazz and Southern cuisine hot spot, in West Oak Lane. Then they opened Green Soul, serving healthy comfort food in a fast-casual setting.

Left: South.

Right: Warmdaddy's.

A year later the Bynums opened South, a beautifully decorated restaurant with three unique spaces—a jazz cub, a dining room, and a bar/lounge with an extensive American bourbon and whiskey program. South attracts local and national acts that earned it a place on *DownBeat* magazine's list of great jazz venues. With South, they aren't far from their roots; their newest restaurant is located on North Broad Street in an emerging neighborhood just twelve miles south of where Cadillac Lounge and Impulse once stood.

Warmdaddy's
1400 S. Columbus Blvd., 215-462-2000

warmdaddys.com

Relish
7152 Ogontz Ave., 215-276-0170

relishphiladelphia.com

Green Soul
1410 Mt. Vernon St., 215-660-9600

greensoulliving.com

South
600 N. Broad St., 215-600-0200

southrestaurant.net

PHILADELPHIA'S CHINATOWN

For a taste of Asia

In the late 1840s, civil war and economic stagnation plagued China, while the U.S. was rumored to have an abundance of well-paying jobs. Chinese laborers set off for America, but instead of prosperity, they found discriminatory laws and poverty. Over time they fanned out across the country, opening businesses and creating thriving Asian communities. In 1871, Philadelphia's Chinatown was born when Lee Fong opened a laundry at 913 Race Street. A few other Chinese businesses opened nearby, but it was another hundred years before the area really started to grow and businesses catering to immigrants from other East Asian countries started opening in the area.

Chinatown encompasses the area from the Vine Street Expressway south to Arch Street and from 8th to 11th Streets, abutting the Reading Terminal Market (see page 148) and the Pennsylvania Convention Center. The forty-foot-tall Chinese Friendship Gate serves as a grand entrance to the neighborhood. Wok'N Walk Tours of Chinatown (see page 176) start at the Friendship Gate.

The bustling neighborhood provides a taste of Hong Kong, China, Taiwan, Korea, Thailand, Malaysia, Burma, and Vietnam. The neighborhood is crowded with residents, local Philadelphians, conventioneers, and tourists seeking out well-established restaurants, such as Dim Sum Garden with its open kitchen and beloved soup dumplings; Penang, serving Malaysian cuisine in a hip industrial setting; Ray's Café and Tea House, known for its siphon coffee; and Rangoon, serving a large selection of Burmese cuisine, including homemade thousand-layer bread. The newest trend, Thai ice cream, also called stir-fried ice cream or simply fried ice cream, is gaining

Left: Ray's Café & Tea House. Photo by Irene Levy Baker.

Right: Chinese Friendship Gate. Photo by Irene Levy Baker.

traction in Chinatown. The dessert is made by pouring milk over a frozen grill, mixing in fruits, candies, or flavors, rolling it up, and serving several rolls standing in a cup. It is often topped with syrup and candies.

Another popular newcomer is Chinatown Square, an uber-modern Asian food hall with offerings from Thailand to Korea with a detour to Mexico and capped off with a cool bar with entertainment and private karaoke rooms. It's open until the wee hours of the morning for drinking and late-night snacks.

Dim Sum Garden
1020 Race St., 215-873-0258

dimsumgardenphilly.com

Penang
117 N. 10th St., 215-413-2531

Ray's Café & Tea House
141 N. 9th St., 215-922-5122

rayscafe.com

Rangoon
112 N. 9th St., 215-829-8939

rangoonphilly.com

Chinatown Square
1016-1018 Race St.

facebook.com/chinatownsquare

Meals that will go down in history

After touring Philadelphia's historic sights, the best way to stay immersed in history is to feast at City Tavern, which was inspired by the customs and foods of eighteenth century Colonial America. The tavern serves lunch and dinner, and carries a full line of beers using the founding fathers' recipes and other libations.

The original City Tavern was the unofficial meeting place of delegates to the first Continental Congress, which convened at nearby Carpenter's Hall. It also served as a prisoner of war camp for Continental and British troops and for three days in 1877 the official headquarters of the Continental Army under General George Washington. Paul Revere stopped at City Tavern on his ride from Boston, and George Washington stopped by both as a general and newly elected president.

The original tavern burned down in 1834 and was later razed. A historically accurate replica reopened for the country's bicentennial celebration in 1976, after painstaking research by the National Park Service using period images, written accounts, and insurance surveys. The tavern appears essentially as it did two hundred years earlier.

Walter Staib, chef/owner of City Tavern since 1994, takes great

DON'T MISS: Colonial Turkey Pot Pie—a hearty pie brimming with turkey, mushrooms, peas, potatoes, sherry cream sauce, and accompanied by Pennsylvania Dutch egg noodles and the Raspberry Shrub, which is raspberry juice vinegar sweetened with sugar and spiked with alcohol or fizzed with soda water. Often served in City Tavern's lovely garden.

Top right: City Tavern's Colonial Turkey Pot Pie.

Above left: City Tavern.

Above right: Walter Staib, chef/owner, City Tavern.

pride in providing authentic eighteenth century-style gourmet cuisine. Staib is a third-generation restaurateur as well as an author, Emmy Award-winning TV host, James Beard-nominated chef, and culinary historian.

138 S. 2nd St., 215-413-1443

citytavern.com

PIZZA BRAIN & MUSEUM

World's largest collection of pizza memorabilia

Imagine walking into a pizza place and seeing a pizza named after you. That could happen to Bob Shieldsmoose or Felix Hupert. When Pizza Brain's owner worked in data entry, he collected unusual names, and they found a home at this quirky pizzeria. The names are quirky, the pies are quirky, and the place is quirky but not so quirky (or maybe just quirky enough) to be noticed by *The New York Times*, *Condé Nast Traveler*, Food Network, and many others.

The Bob Shieldsmoose is topped with pulled brisket, Maytag bleu cheese, garlic, horseradish, black pepper, mozzarella, and rosemary. If not for the crust, it would taste like a Passover seder in one pizza pie. The Lucy Waggle is topped with mozzarella, Grana Padano (a hard cheese), pine nuts, fresh thyme, dates, prosciutto, and arugula. The pizzas are cooked in a gas-fired, brick-lined oven using the best available ingredients, including fresh herbs. There is a tiny dining area inside and another out back, where one wall is covered with a pizza mural and the other in a mosaic mural by Philadelphia artist Isaiah Zagar.

DON'T MISS: Little Baby's Ice Cream, the attached ice cream parlor that is dedicated to making "the best and weirdest ice cream in the world." It is fulfilling its mission with such flavors as pizza and ants on a log (celery, peanut butter, and raisins), and a weird opening day video that went viral, attracting more than twelve million views.

Left: Pizza Brain mural.

Right: The Bob Shieldsmoose. Photo by David Baker.

Inside is founder Brian James Dwyer's shrine to pizza. Called the Pizza Museum, it holds the Guinness World Record for being the world's largest (and perhaps only) collection of pizza memorabilia. The walls of the 150-year-old row house are covered in pizza games, pizza-themed Barbie dolls, toys, comic books, vintage posters, framed magazine covers, pizza advertisements and pizza-esque records, and action figures.

It's a must-see destination that's a feast for the mouth and the eyes.

Pizza Brain

2313 Frankford Ave., 215-291-2965

pizzabrain.org

Little Baby's Ice Cream

2311 Frankford Ave., 267-687-8567

4903 Catharine St., 215-921-2100

littlebabysicecream.com

And other great brunch spots

In 1994, in honor of what would have been William Penn's 350th birthday, an artist was commissioned to paint the compass in the center of the courtyard at Philadelphia City Hall. That artist was David Salama, a native Bolivian with a degree in art, who went on to open Crêperie Beau Monde. The man who commissioned the piece was legendary City Planner Edmund Bacon, who is also the father of actor Kevin Bacon.

With all that bacon around, perhaps it's not surprising that Salama's restaurant is one of Philadelphia's top brunch spots.

Salama and business partner, Jim Caiola, own Crêperie Beau Monde, a romantic Beaux-Arts-style bistro in Queen Village. The duo uses authentic flat, round cast-iron griddles imported from Brittany to make savory and sweet crepes such as Pan-Seared Duck Breast, Brie, and Black Mission Fig Jam or Pears, Goat Cheese, Creme Fraîche, and Lavender Honey.

624 S. 6th St., 215-592-0656

creperie-beaumonde.com

Other brunch hotspots include:

Day By Day
2101 Sansom St., 215-564-5540

daybydayinc.com

Traditional brunch dishes plus outstanding breads and bakery items.

Green Eggs Cafe
719 N. 2nd St., 215-922-3447

1306 Dickinson St., 215-226-3447

212 S. 13th St.

greeneggscafe.com

Hearty servings of brunch foods served daily until 4:00 p.m.

Left: The recently restored compass in the center of City Hall. Photo provided by the Office of Art, Culture & the Creative Economy.

Right: Beau Monde. Photo by Michael Perisco.

Honey's Sit N Eat

2101 South St., 215-732-5130

800 N. 4th St., 215-925-1150

honeyssitneat.com

Southern comfort food meets Jewish deli at this homey restaurant.

Hungry Pigeon

hungrypigeon.com

An all-day cafe with exceptional pastries and coffee. (See page 68)

Parc Restaurant, Bistro & Cafe

parc-restaurant.com

Stephen Starr's French bistro, with outside tables on Rittenhouse Square, makes every meal feel like an occasion. (See page 200)

Sabrina's Café

901 Christian St., 215-574-1599

1804 Callowhill St., 215-636-9061

227 N. 34th St., 215-222-1022

50 E. Wynnewood Rd. Wynnewood, PA, 484-412-8790

714 Haddon Ave. Collingswood, NJ, 856-214-0723

sabrinascafe.com

Serves brunch daily until 3:00 p.m. All BYOB except University City.

From Italian Market to East Passyunk's Restaurant Row

Strolling along 9th Street between Fitzwater and Wharton awakens the senses. The smell of spices and fish. The sight of tables overflowing with fruits and vegetables that spill out onto the sidewalk. The sounds of commerce, busy streets, and live chickens. The tastes of the freshly made pasta, spices, olives, cheese, and cannoli in the small, mostly family-owned shops and the many classic Italian trattorias and newer restaurants in the neighborhood.

It's been that way since 1884 when Antonio Palumbo opened a boarding house for fellow Italian immigrants. A few businesses cropped up in the neighborhood to serve the burgeoning Italian community, and it grew to become the country's largest outdoor market. This is not a spanking-clean food court but a working market full of tiny shops. Many have been family owned for generations and conduct business in front of shoppers, giving it a bustling old-school feel. While many longtime shops remain (see Di Bruno Bros. on page 60, Fante's on page 172, Pat's King of Steaks and Geno's Steaks on page 156), new waves of immigrants have made their mark on 9th Street, including Mexicans, Koreans, and Vietnamese. Visit on your own or take a guided tour.

Pat's King of Steaks and Geno's Steaks (see page 156) anchor the Italian Market at the intersection of 9th Street, Wharton Street, and East Passyunk Avenue. Going southeast on Passyunk, one of the few diagonal streets to interrupt Philadelphia's logical grid-patterned streets, leads to one of Philadelphia's most exciting restaurant rows. East Passyunk is home to Brigantessa, Fond, Noord, Laurel, and ITV (see page 190), Townsend (see page 186), Capogiro Gelato Artisans (see page 134), Mr. Martino's Trattoria (see page 30), Bing Bing Dim

Top: Historic photo of the Italian Market. Courtesy of Fante's.

Above left: Italian Market dried fruit. Photo by Paulcheney.com.

Above right: Italian Market. Photo by Paulcheney.com.

Sum (see page 78), Barcelona Wine Bar, Saté Kampar (see page 44), Will BYOB (see page 4), and Le Virtù. All are independently and locally owned except Barcelona, and it's not unusual to find their chefs shopping at the Italian Market.

9th St. Italian Market
S. 9th St. between Wharton and Fitzwater, 215-278-2903
italianmarketphilly.org

Italian Market Immersion
by Philadelphia Urban Adventures
215-280-3746
urbanadventures.com/italian-market-immersion

Taste4Travel Tour
610-506-6120
taste4travel.net

From cigars to chestnuts

In 1975, Manny Radbill, a cigar salesman, decided that it was time for a career change and convinced Howard Bernstein, his son-in-law, that it wasn't nuts to open a nut store. Bernstein, whose grandfather and great-grandfather owned the now-closed Levis Hot Dogs, liked the idea. He had worked at Levis, an iconic Philadelphia eatery, over the summers and felt he had retail in his blood.

The father and his son-in-law opened their first Nuts To You location on 20th Street between Market and Chestnut Streets, a neighborhood that at the time was populated by many panhandlers and homeless people. The duo was generous with their nuts and snacks, giving them a chance to get to know John, a quiet, respectful homeless man who typically wore military fatigues. The Vietnam veteran made it clear that he wasn't a beggar but wanted to work for his food. So they hired him to clean the shop. He did so with a passion, arriving early six days a week, lifting heavy bags of nuts, and volunteering to spend days on his back cleaning the mesh roaster with a toothpick and keeping the shop clean. John worked there for more than ten years. That's not unusual at Nuts To You, where several employees have worked for decades.

In the years since, the neighborhood around the first location has started buzzing with business executives and residents who browse the no-frills shop for bags of nuts, nut mixes, seeds, grains, dried fruit, chocolates, candies, coffee, tea, and snack mixes. Popcorn is their No. 1 best-seller, and they have twelve different types of almonds alone—salted, roasted, smoked, and covered with everything from Tamari to extra dark chocolate to pumpkin-flavored yogurt.

Radbill has retired, and the third generation has entered the family business. His grandson, Justin, remembers at age five or six standing

Top left: Howard and Justin Bernstein. Used with permission of *The Philadelphia Inquirer*. Copyright ©2017. All rights reserved.

Top right: Interior. Photo by Adrian Castillo, Associate Creative Director, Brownstein Group.

Above: Justin Bernstein. Photo by Adrian Castillo, Associate Creative Director, Brownstein Group.

on a step stool to push the buttons on the cash register. Even then he knew he wanted to join his father and grandfather in the family business.

Nuts To You has grown from one location to five, has a thriving online business, and is now run by the third generation of the family. That's the story . . . in a nutshell.

22-24 S. 20th St., 215-567-7330

1328 Walnut St., 215-545-2911

1500 Market St., 215-271-1644

721 Walnut St., 215-925-1141

10861 Bustleton Ave., Northeast Philly, 215-677-8520

nuts-to-you.com

JAPANESE TEA CEREMONY

Carefully choreographed to capture all senses

The Japanese tea ceremony, called *chanoyu* or *chado*, has been practiced for more than 450 years. It's an art form, spiritual discipline, and a way to socialize designed to be profoundly touching. It can take years of training to learn not only the etiquette involved but also how to be fully present in the moment engaging the heart and all of the senses. Don't expect a dramatic presentation but rather a subtle ceremony that focuses on sharing and is designed to help participants appreciate a moment that will never come again. Watching the demonstration by practitioners from the Chado Urasenke Tankokai Philadelphia Association is a window into Japanese culture, and, if you allow it, the carefully choreographed presentation quietly works its way into your heart.

Tea ceremony demonstrations are held April through October in the Shofuso Japanese House and Garden. A "host" and a "guest" wearing traditional kimonos act out the ceremony, while a live narrator with a sonorous voice explains the subtle actions and the many nuances to the audience. The narrator explains the care with which the tea bowl and utensils are chosen, the bowing, and the polite questions and traditional responses between the host and guest.

The audience sits on the floor in a U-shape around the ceremony. It's traditional for audience members to sit on their knees, but sidesaddle or cross-legged is also acceptable. (Placing feet straight out, is not.) Chairs are available upon request. While the narrator, host, and guest wear traditional kimonos, observers may dress casually. Advanced registration is necessary, as ceremonies regularly sell out. Observers are asked to remove their shoes at the door and can wear nylon peds, which are provided, or socks.

After watching the intricate ritual, which lasts about forty-five minutes, everyone in the audience is presented with a traditional

Top: Japanese Tea Ceremony exterior. Photo courtesy of Japan America of Greater Philadelphia.

Above left and right: Japanese Tea Ceremony Photos courtesy of Japan America of Greater Philadelphia.

seasonal Japanese sweet and a bowl of green matcha tea. The sweet is eaten just before drinking the tea to counterbalance the bitter taste. The demonstration concludes with a question and answer session.

The Shofuso Japanese Tea House's sliding doors open to the beautiful seventeenth century–style Japanese garden, with a koi pond, weeping cherry trees, and waterfalls. Plan to arrive early or stay late to walk around the house and 1.2-acre gardens.

Horticultural and Lansdowne Drives
West Fairmount Park, 215-878-5097
japanesehouse.org

Tall ship with a sailor at her helm

The *Moshulu* is the world's oldest and largest square-rigged sailing vessel still afloat and the world's only restaurant on a tall ship. Built in 1904, the three-thousand-ton ship was originally dubbed *Kurt* by her German owners. She carried coal, nitrate, coke, and other products around Cape Horn more than fifty times without incident. During World War I, the ship was confiscated by the U.S. Navy, which renamed her *Dreadnaught*. Later, Mrs. Woodrow Wilson renamed her *Moshulu*, a Native American word for "one who fears nothing." In the ensuing years, the ship had many more successful voyages until World War II when the Nazis confiscated her and stripped her of her masts and spars. She was then retired and used for storage until she was restored and moved to Philadelphia in 1974. After several fits and starts, a fire, and a change of owners, she reopened as a restaurant called the Moshulu in 2002.

Though she no longer sails the world, the *Moshulu* still has a sailor at its helm. Anthony Bonett has been executive chef of the Moshulu since 2011 after honing his skills at some of Philadelphia's finest restaurants and in the U.S. Navy. After attending Temple University, Bonett enlisted in the Navy, serving aboard the aircraft carrier, USS *Forrestal*, but he wasn't serving food. He was dishing up weather reports. While Bonett was a weatherman on the ship, he also worked in the ship's kitchen, cooking for five thousand sailors, the admiral, and his executive staff. His ship traveled throughout the Mediterranean, where he learned about different cuisines.

Three days after finishing his tour of duty, Bonett traded his white naval uniform for chef's whites. He enrolled in The Restaurant School at Walnut Hill College. Later that day he put on a civilian suit and walked into what he was told was the best restaurant in the city—the Fountain at the Four Seasons, Philadelphia—and got an

Top right: Moshulu exterior. Photo by Allison Guzy.

Above left: Executive Chef Anthony Bonett.

Above right: *Moshulu*. Photo by Allison Guzy.

internship in the kitchen of Jean-Marie LaCroix, one of the city's culinary pioneers. Ironically, his path through some of Philadelphia's top kitchens led him back to a ship—the *Moshulu*.

The *Moshulu* cuts a majestic figure docked on Philadelphia's Delaware River, where diners have Instagram-worthy views of the Ben Franklin Bridge, the waterfront, and the skyline, and the former sailor at its helm serves classic American cuisine with Mediterranean and Asian flavors.

401 S. Columus Blvd., 215-923-2500

moshulu.com

The scoop on the city's best ice cream

When Mr. and Mrs. Berley decided to decorate their dining room like an old-fashioned ice cream parlor complete with wire-back chairs, stained glass, and an old peanut roaster, they probably never dreamed that they were foreshadowing their sons' future.

All those family trips to flea markets and antique stores and historic sites to acquire the ice cream fountain furnishings had a lasting impact. Ryan followed his mother's footsteps into the antique business but was growing restless. At a family dinner one night, Ryan threw out the idea of opening an ice cream parlor on the ground floor of a historic building the family was renovating.

Ryan's brother Eric was about to go back to his philosophy studies at College of William & Mary but had no particular plans after graduation. The more the brothers thought about it, the better they liked the plan, and the location was perfect. Not only was it in the historic district, but it was also full of wonderful details, such as a ceiling and walls covered in decorative tin and a porcelain mosaic tile floor. Their parents, who had been collecting antiques since their honeymoon, also had two barns full of antiques to offer.

In 2004, they opened the ice cream parlor, which they named The Franklin Fountain, after Ben Franklin, Philadelphia's favorite son. The family's love of antiques can be seen from the marble fountain to the copper pots. The brothers even grew period-appropriate mustaches and create throwback flavors, such as Hydrox Cookie and Teaberry Gum.

Soon after opening, the soda fountain started to attract both praise and lines out the door. *Food & Wine* named The Franklin Fountain one of the best soda fountains in the country, specifically mentioning its devotion to history, and *USA Today* called its milkshakes the best in the country. Food Network ranked the Mt. Vesuvius sundae—

Left: Franklin Fountain by Vicki Liantonio.

Right: Berley Brothers—photo of Eric (left) and Ryan Berley taken using the collodion process, a photographic process introduced during the 1850s. Photo by Michael Bartolotta. Courtesy of Shane Confectionery.

with its mountain of ice cream erupting in chocolate brownie boulders, cascading with hot fudge, and blanketed with malt powder with a dollop of whipped cream as a smoke signal—one of the top five ice creams in America.

The brothers have added two more sweet eateries on the same block—Shane Confectionery in 2011 and Franklin Ice Cream Bar in 2018 (see page 108) —showing they can lick the candy business too.

116 Market St., 215-627-1899

franklinfountain.com

SHANE CONFECTIONERY

The oldest continuously operating confectionery in the country

The storefront at 110 Market Street is no rookie when it comes to candy. Confectioners have been occupying this sweet address since 1863. At first it was a wholesale candy business, and then it was taken over in 1911 by the Shane family and became a full-blown candy store. The location was in the path of tens of thousands of buttercream-loving commuters taking the ferry from Philadelphia across the Delaware River to Camden. Over ninety-nine years, three generations of the Shane family weathered the opening of the Ben Franklin Bridge, which cut into foot traffic in the area, a sugar shortage brought on by World War II, and a changing neighborhood. Eventually, the candy shop had seen sweeter days, and the family had run out of heirs.

Eric and Ryan Berley, who own The Franklin Fountain (see page 106), a vintage ice cream fountain a few doors away, took over the business in 2011. The Berley brothers preserved the name and learned about clear toy candy, a Pennsylvania German delicacy made with sugar, water, corn syrup, and food coloring. They collected hundreds of cast-iron molds for the edible candies, including animals, boats, and trains. The antique-loving brothers took the candy store back to its heyday, lovingly restoring the decor, with its rounded glass-front windows topped with stained glass, old–

DON'T MISS: The Berley brothers' newest sweet shop – Franklin Ice Cream Bar, specializing in keystone shaped ice cream bars dipped in chocolate roasted at Shane Confectionery and sprinkled in candy.

Left: Shane Chocolate. Courtesy of Shane Confectionery.

Right: Shane Confectionary interior. Photo courtesy of Shane Confectionery.

fashioned candy jars, turn-of-the-century cash registers, and tin ceiling. Besides the chocolate-covered caramels, buttercreams, fruit slices, fudge and, seasonally, clear toy candies, there's an inviting hot chocolate/milkshake bar. The confectionery's signature Whirly Berley Bar is made of salted chocolate caramel and honey nougat dunked in dark chocolate and sprinkled with cocoa nibs.

Shane Confectionery periodically offers behind-the-scenes tours providing information about the candy shop's history and decor as well as a look at the chocolate-making machines, the collection of more than a thousand clear toy candy molds, and, of course, samples.

Shane Confectionery

110 Market St., 215-922-1048

shanecandies.com

Franklin Ice Cream Bar

112 Market St., 215-967-1184

franklinicecream.com

CULINARY LITERACY CENTER

What's cooking at Free Library of Philadelphia

You might expect to find cookbooks at the Free Library of Philadelphia, but you'd be surprised to find a commercial-grade kitchen. The kitchen, which opened in 2014, is like a culinary classroom—advancing literacy with a fork and knife.

At the Culinary Literacy Center, the kitchen becomes the classroom, teaching math by measuring, reading through recipes, and basic science by baking. Nutrition, health, culture, and history are folded into the lessons. In the kitchen, non-native English speakers can hone their language skills, and adult literacy students can refine their reading. Classes are available for library patrons of all ages and needs, from preschoolers through senior citizens, veterans, and even people who are blind. All classes involve tastings, and many are free or low cost.

The programs have been so successful that the staff has created a "Class in a Box" that enables branch libraries in the neighborhoods to host cooking classes, even with limited or no cooking facilities. The box contains instructions, utensils, ingredients, and everything else the instructor needs.

Classes are also offered by Philadelphia chefs, featuring cooking demonstrations followed by a three-course meal with drinks. A list of upcoming classes can be found on the library's website.

Free Library of Philadelphia
1901 Vine St., 4th floor, 215-686-5322
freelibrary.org/cook

Top: Chef Marc Vetri (see page 146) teaching at the Free Library of Philadelphia's Culinary Literacy Center. Photo courtesy of the Free Library of Philadelphia.

Above left: Culinary Literacy Center. Photo courtesy of the Free Library of Philadelphia.

Above right: Culinary Literacy Center. Photo courtesy of the Free Library of Philadelphia.

KAPLAN'S NEW MODEL BAKERY

The city's oldest Jewish bakery

Neither the Atkins diet nor a changing neighborhood nor even a fire can stop Philadelphia's oldest Jewish bakery. Kaplan's New Model Bakery has been making rye bread and challah using the same techniques and recipes for more than a century.

When the bakery opened in 1906, the Northern Liberties neighborhood was full of Eastern European Jews who flocked there for its kosher breads and sweets. These days those flocking to the bakery range from old ladies to young artsy types looking for natural foods plus Ukrainian and Polish immigrants. The bread is also distributed to delis, gourmet shops, and restaurants in the tri-state area.

Over the years, the neighborhood has changed, but the recipes haven't.

Kaplan's is the only Jewish bakery in Philadelphia still making its rye bread using perpetual sour dough, where some of each batch is saved as starter for the next batch. No preservatives or artificial ingredients are used—just rye flour, white flour, water, yeast, and salt, and each challah is hand-twisted using six strands of dough.

In May 2017, one of the ovens burst into flames, but that was just a blip in the bakery's long history. At that point, Stan Silverman and Jeff Solomon had owned the bakery for nearly thirty years. Before that, it was in the hands of the Lipkin family—J.J., his son, Leonard, and his grandson, John. Before buying Kaplan's in the mid-1950s, J.J. founded Gold Medal Rye Bread, which closed after he sold it to

Top right: Kaplan's. Photo by Irene Levy Baker.

Above left: Stan Kaplan braiding challah.

Above right: Kaplan's interior.

an out-of-state firm that changed its recipes. Maybe it's the bakery's insistence on using the tried-and-true recipes and old-school methods that have been the secret to its one-hundred-plus year survival. Or maybe it's just that the bread tastes really, really good.

901 N. Third St., 215-627-5288
kaplansnewmodelbakery.com

Phoenix rising from the ashes

It took two and a half years to lovingly design Maison 208, a two-story restaurant in Midtown Village/The Gayborhood. Meanwhile, on the attached six-story building next door, Mural Arts Philadelphia, whose work has earned the city the status of Mural Capital of the World, was installing a work that was visible above the restaurant. Then the nearly finished restaurant and mural were destroyed in a fire that was later determined to be a case of arson.

Chef Sylva Senat and owner Herb Reid were determined to rebuild and repaint despite the setback. It took another year, but the new incarnation was even more beautiful than the original. Artist James Burns re-created the mural, called *Sanctuary*, which is a whimsical piece enlivened by woodpeckers, orioles, and other birds. They were so enamored with the mural that they asked Burns to enlarge it. The mural now starts on the wall of the six-story building next door, where it can be seen above the restaurant and continues along the inside wall of the restaurant's second floor bar and down to the ground floor. Thanks to a retractable roof—the city's first—the ceiling above the second floor bar can open, providing an unobstructed view of the mural and further incorporating it into the

DON'T MISS: *Sanctuary* was created through Mural Arts' Porch Light program, an ongoing collaboration with the Department of Behavioral Health and disAbility Services. The mural is part of the Community Wellness Project in partnership with Broad Street Ministry and is designed to raise awareness about mental and emotional health and inspire conversation about community health.

Left: The second floor rooftop bar with mural on right.

Right: Chef Sylva Senat.

atmosphere. Floor-to-ceiling windows on the north and east sides of the restaurant's first floor can also be opened to let in a breeze. The birds in the mural became a design element inspiring the use of antique bird cages in the funky light fixtures and names of the cocktails.

The New American cuisine is as sophisticated as the decor. Senat is a kitchen-trained chef from Haiti whose dishes start with French foundations mixed with bold Caribbean flavors and spices. His skills earned him stints at Tashan (now-closed), Buddakan (see page 200) in Philadelphia and New York City, Aquavit, and Jean-Georges, and even a place on the 14th season of Bravo's *Top Chef*. Maison 208 is also known for its natural wines, beer list, and craft cocktails, including the gin & terrarium, a one-of-a-kind cocktail actually served in a terrarium.

Perhaps the early misfortune at Maison 208 was a sign that the restaurant in the heart of Midtown Village/The Gayborhood was destined to be hot!

208 S. 13th St., 215-999-1020

maison208.com

COOK *Photo by Yoni Nimrod* (page 62)

DIZENGOFF *Photo by Michael Persico (page 48)*

OYSTER HOUSE *Photo by Jason Varney* (page 66)

SATÉ KAMPAR *Photo by Kerry McIntyre (page 44)*

MAISON 208 *Photo by Steve Weinik for Mural Arts Philadelphia ©2016 Mural Arts Philadelphia / James Burns / 208 S. 13th St. Reprinted by permission. (page 114)*

MCGILLIN'S OLDE ALE HOUSE *Photo by Thomas Robert Clarke* (page 12)

SURAYA *Photo by Melissa Alam (page 58)*

ITALIAN MARKET *Photo by Paul Cheney Jr. - paulcheney.com (page 98)*

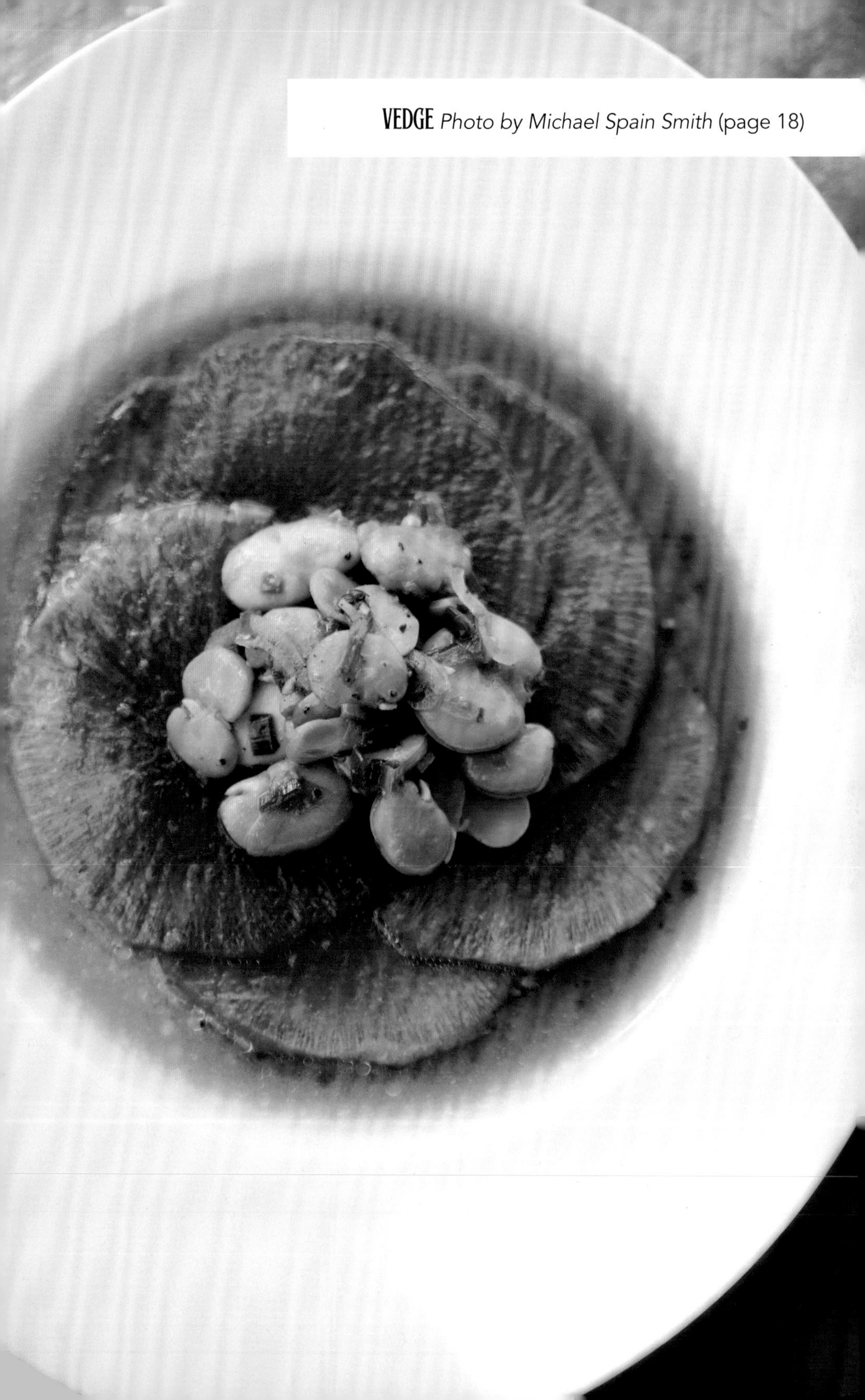

VEDGE *Photo by Michael Spain Smith* (page 18)

WM. MULHERIN'S SONS *Photo by Matthew Williams (page 164)*

JAPANESE TEA GARDEN *Photo courtesy of Japan America of Greater Philadelphia (page 102)*

EL COMPADRE *Photo by Ted Nghiem* (page 54)

DI BRUNO BROS. (page 60)

BASSETTS ICE CREAM (page 24)

GOOD SPOON *Photo by Ryan Scott* (page 74)

Licking the details

Stephanie Reitano carries a leather-bound book with her wherever she goes. Throughout the day, she fills the blank pages with her tiny handwritten lists of things to do. Next to each item is a tiny box to check when it is completed.

You could say that Reitano is a bit of a perfectionist, and that's good news for gelato lovers because she's also that detail oriented when she selects the ingredients that go into Capogiro Gelato Artisans' products. She controls everything, from the type of cows that produce the milk to the pasteurization process, creating pure flavors that have earned accolades from national publications.

National Geographic called Capogiro the No. 1 Ice Cream Spot in the World. The magazine specifically called out the Madagascar bourbon vanilla, Saigon cinnamon, and Thai coconut milk, as well as flavors featuring pomegranate, hazelnut, and pumpkin, and *The New York Times* raved about the sea salt gelato.

Reitano's gelato is made daily in small batches. It starts with raw milk from grass-fed Scottish Ayrshire cows at one of two farms in Honeybrook, Pennsylvania, and Reitano says she can tell the season by tasting the milk. She pasteurizes it herself and creates four bases—white, yellow (with egg yolks), chocolate, and sugar—then flavors it with fruits, herbs, cream, and eggs. Anything that can be produced locally she purchases from Green Meadows Farm in Gap, Pennsylvania, allowing the freshly picked fruit to ripen on the vine rather than on a truck, and then she roasts or poaches the fruit in-house. She has created more than four hundred flavors.

The gelateria offers a rotating list of thirty flavors at a time. The gelato is beautifully displayed and garnished as it is in Italian gelaterias. Reitano "discovered" gelato on a fifth anniversary trip there, with her husband, John, who was born in Italy. She fell in love

Left: Gelato. Photo by Lexy Pierce.

Right: Capogiro flavors. Photo by Irene Levy Baker.

with the creamy dessert and came home determined to master the art of making it. She certainly succeeded!

All those little items scrawled on Reitano's to-do list add up to big flavors in Capogiro's noteworthy gelato.

119 S. 13th St., 215-351-0900
117 S. 20th St., 215-636-9250
1625 E. Passyunk Ave., 215-462-3790

Capofritto Pizzeria & Gelateria
233 Chestnut St., 215-897-9999
capogirogelato.com

DON'T MISS: The black raspberry gelato. If you're lucky enough to see it, get it, because it's only available for a week or two in July when the berries are in season.

FARMER'S KEEP AND SWEET FREEDOM

Allergy-free restaurants

Josh Bullock was pretty excited on the night he opened his restaurant. His five-year-old nephew was even more excited, especially when he realized that he could eat *anything* in the place. That was big news for the little boy who had recently been rushed to the hospital because of a food allergy. His mother, Bullock's sister, also has food allergies.

Bullock thought of how many of a family's most intimate moments—weddings, holidays, funerals, wakes—revolve around food. He felt no one should be excluded. That inspired him to open Farmer's Keep, which is gluten free, dairy free, egg free, nut free (tree nuts and peanuts), and shellfish free. It's a safe place for his sister, his nephew, and anyone with the six most common food allergies. In fact, in 2017, Food Allergy Research and Education (FARE), one of the world's leading food allergy groups, named Farmer's Keep the Business of the Year.

But it's not just for diners with allergies. The healthy, creative cuisine appeals to anyone who wants a good meal, and because diners pay by the weight of their meal, they can control their portion sizes, which is another plus for those with bigger or smaller appetites. The restaurant also has a bottle shop with more than two hundred craft beers.

The concept for Sweet Freedom Bakery also grew from a familial experience with food allergies. Early in her career, when Alison Lubert was counseling college students, she took a holistic approach to their mental health, talking to them about their sleep habits, diet, and alcohol consumption. She always had an interest in nutrition and that was compounded when her husband and son were both

Left: Sweet Freedom cupcakes.

Right: Roasted root vegetables and seeds with a garlic dressing at Farmer's Keep.

diagnosed with food allergies. After much trial-and-error baking, with her husband as a willing taste tester, she opened Sweet Freedom, Philadelphia's first gluten free, vegan, allergy friendly bakery.

The cakes, cookies, cupcakes, muffins, donuts, and breads are vegan, dairy free, casein free, egg free, gluten free, and kosher and do not contain refined sugar, corn, wheat, peanuts, or soy. The baked goods look and taste so great that they made it onto Food Network's *Cupcake Wars* their first year. The bakery has since expanded to the suburbs.

Farmer's Keep
10 S. 20th St., 215-309-2928
farmerskeep.com

Sweet Freedom
1424 South St., 215-545-1899
1039 W. Lancaster Ave., Bryn Mawr, 610-527-7323
sweetfreedombakery.com

Other Gluten Free Restaurants/Bakeries

Bassetts Ice Cream (see page 24)
Reading Terminal Market, 51 N.12th St., 215-925-4315
bassettsicecream.com

Most flavors are gluten free.

Cheu Noodle Bar, Cheu Fishtown, Bing Bing Dim Sum
(see page 78)
Dishes that are gluten free or can be gluten free are marked on menus.

Citizens Bank Park
(Open during Phillies games)
One Citizens Bank Way, 215-463-1000
mlb.com/phillies

Many gluten free options

The Happy Mixer
4275 County Line Road, Chalfont, PA, 267-663-7209
Ferry Market, 32 S. Main St., New Hope, PA, 267-664-4886
12 Summit Square, Langhorne, PA, 215-860-1989
thehappymixer.com

Gluten free, vegan bakery with dairy free, egg and soy free options. No high fructose corn syrup or trans fats.

P.S. & Co.
1706 Locust St., 215-985-1706
puresweets.com

All dishes are organic plant based and gluten free.

Posh Pop Bakeshop
109 Kings Highway East, Haddonfield, NJ, 856-428-7674
poshpopbakeshop.com

Specializing in gluten free and wheat free baked goods.

Sciascia Confections (see page 178)
sciasciaconfections.com

All of the candies and baked goods are gluten free.

Top right: Farmer's Keep exterior.

Above left: Josh Bullock, owner of Farmer's Keep.

Above right: Manorack and Sunny Phanthavong of Vientiane Café.

Taffets Bakery & Store

1024 S. 9th Street, 215-551-5511

taffets.com

Gluten-free, artisan bakery and store in the heart of the Italian Market.

Victor Cafe (see page 140)

Menu items that are gluten free or can be prepared gluten free
are marked on the menu.

Vientiane Café (see page 32)

Offers many gluten free dishes.

DON'T MISS: Vientiane Bistro, opening in East Kensington in 2018. The menu will feature traditional Laos cuisine, plus gluten free and vegan options.

Music to diners' ears

John DiStefano left Italy for Philadelphia in 1908. Ten years later he was able to open a gramophone shop that served espresso, spumoni, and a steady diet of music. DiStefano was passionate about classical music and grand opera and soon developed relationships with performers as well as the directors at nearby RCA Records. He ended up introducing RCA executives to many budding artists, including Alfred Cocozza, who became a legendary tenor, known as Mario Lanza. A museum dedicated to his career, the Mario Lanza Institute and Museum is about a mile from Victor Cafe.

After Prohibition, DiStefano purchased a liquor license, and his shop became a full-fledged restaurant. As he aged, John relied on his sons, Armand and Henry, to run the business. Henry became the sole proprietor in 1954 and passed the restaurant down to his wife and children, John's grandchildren.

Today, Victor Cafe serves traditional Italian cuisine and wine on red-and-white checkered tablecloths. The walls are adorned with signed photos and opera memorabilia, and diners with a taste for opera are serenaded every twenty minutes or so by professional opera singers and students moonlighting as servers.

1303 Dickinson St., 215-468-3040
victorcafe.com

Top right: Victor Cafe interior. Photo by Irene Levy Baker.

Above left: Toffer Mihalka performing at Victor Cafe. Photo by Marianne Prager.

Above right: The cozy upstairs bar at Victor Cafe. Photo by Irene Levy Baker.

DON'T MISS: Victor Cafe in the movies *Rocky Balboa*, *Creed* and *Creed II*. In the movies, it was a restaurant owned and operated by Rocky, called Adrian's. During the film shoots, boxing photos and pictures of Adrian, the character's late wife, were interspersed between the opera paraphernalia on the walls of the restaurant.

Big things are brewing

Todd Carmichael, cofounder and CEO of La Colombe, is an adventurer who is up for a challenge. During his college days, he was a barista at the Seattle cafe that would later become Starbucks. No doubt most people's skills would be tested just making grande skinny half caf mocha frappacinos, but those aren't people who have sailed solo across the Atlantic or walked seven hundred miles across Antarctica to the South Pole in record-breaking speed.

After his barista days, Carmichael spent six years traveling throughout Europe delving into the coffee culture in preparation for his next venture. He set out to not only roast great coffee but also make the world better.

In 1994, Carmichael and his business partner, Jean Philippe "J.P." Iberti, opened the first La Colombe, where they roast responsibly gathered beans using ancient and modern coffee traditions from around the globe. The cafe, located in Philadelphia's Rittenhouse Square, drew such a loyal following that the team opened another cafe in Philadelphia's Fishtown, a hipster neighborhood (see page 74). The industrial-chic eleven-thousand-square-foot Fishtown location serves coffee, plus food and drinks, and is home to roasting facilities and distilling of the company's signature rum. These cafes and each subsequent location are designed to make guests happy—from the temperature of the shop to the music to the mouth feel of the mugs. It has everything except WiFi because the owners want to encourage social interaction, not social media.

To meet the other challenge—doing social good—La Colombe has teamed up with the Leonardo DiCaprio Foundation to create the Lyon Blend, which benefits wildlife and forests, and helps fund clean water projects, disaster relief, and climate change research, and, with the Clinton Foundation, to fund the Haiti Coffee

Left: La Colombe's eleven-thousand-square-foot facility in Fishtown. Courtesy of La Colombe.

Right: Todd Carmichael, co-founder and CEO of La Colombe. Courtesy of La Colombe.

Academy, which is designed to revive the country's coffee industry. The coffee roaster has paired up with ECHOES Around the World in Uganda, Wide Horizons for Children in Ethiopia, and the Rainforest Alliance.

Two decades after Carmichael and Iberti opened the first La Colombe, Hamdi Ulukaya, founder/CEO and chairman of Chobani, became the company's only investor, and the team has gone on to open more coffee houses in Philadelphia; Washington, D.C.; Chicago; Los Angeles; and Boston; and its beans can be found at retailers around the country. Carmichael now hosts the Travel Channel's reality/adventure show *Dangerous Grounds*, which captures his worldwide treks to find coffee beans.

130 S. 19th St. (original location), 215-563-0860
1335 Frankford Ave., 267-479-1600
1414 S. Penn Square, 215-977-7770
100 S. Independence Mall West, 267-479-1650
lacolombe.com

Snacks with a twist

The average American eats one and a half to two pounds of pretzels a year. Philadelphians eat twelve times that amount. Thanks to the Pennsylvania Dutch, these "little rewards" are available from street vendors and food carts throughout the city and at Reading Terminal Market (see page 148), where you can find two popular pretzel variations. You'll find more traditional Philadelphia-style pretzels made by Center City Soft Pretzel at the Pennsylvania General Store and another tasty option nearby at Miller's Twist.

While not exactly the style of pretzel that Philadelphia is known for, the pretzels at Miller's Twist are a finger-licking treat. They are hand-rolled, twisted, dipped in butter, salted, and then served hot and chewy by mostly Amish workers from Lancaster County. The process takes twenty minutes from mixing to mouth. Owner Roger Miller has learned how to make them perfect for any time of the day—from an egg and cheese breakfast pretzel to the pretzel dog, which is filled with an all-beef hot dog. His best-seller remains the original salted pretzel with butter.

Tony Tonelli opened Center City Soft Pretzel Company in the heart of the Italian Market (see page 98) in 1981 despite death threats from a competitor. He not only survived but also thrived, and he plans to pass the business on to his daughter, Erika Tonelli Bonnett. It's a real family affair with Tonelli's grandson, ex-son-in-law, and even ninety-plus-year-old mother all involved in the business.

DON'T MISS: Beiler's Doughnuts. Beiler's was named one of America's 20 best desserts by *Fodor's Travel*. It was one of the first Amish merchants to move into Reading Terminal Market.

Left: Miller's Twist at Reading Terminal Market.

Right: Center City Soft Pretzels.

The pretzels at Center City Soft Pretzel are free of nuts, eggs, dairy, trans fats, preservatives, and additives, and are even kosher. In fact, they are made from just three ingredients—flour, yeast, and water—yet, the simple snack has become an iconic Philadelphia food. Why? Bonnett thinks it's because pretzels can morph into whatever you want them to be. A sprinkle of cinnamon sugar makes them sweet; a dash of cheese makes them savory. Tonelli fondly recalls a mother telling him that a pretzel is an affordable way to keep her children full at school all day, and one of his proudest moments was receiving an order from the Obama campaign for forty thousand pretzels to keep Philadelphians satiated while waiting in line at the polls on election day.

Miller's Twist
Reading Terminal Market, 51 N.12th St., 215-923-1723
millerstwist.com

Center City Soft Pretzel
816 Washington Ave., 215-463-5664
centercitypretzel.com

Award-winning Italian cuisine

When Marc Vetri got his first job washing dishes in Margate, New Jersey, no one would have guessed that three decades later the suburban, guitar-toting teenager would be named to *Food & Wine*'s best new chefs list and earn awards from the James Beard Foundation.

The path took him to Drexel University and then to Italy with $1,500 and an introductory note in his pocket. Vetri, a half-Italian kid from Abington, spent two years working for chefs, line cooks, and winemakers in Sicily, Bergamo, Rome, and Piedmont. He dreamed of bringing an authentic Northern Italian restaurant back to his hometown.

He fulfilled his dream in 1999 when he opened Vetri Cucina, now one of the most respected and influential Italian restaurants in the country. The thirty-two-seat gem lit by custom-made, hand-blown Murano glass chandeliers serves rustic Italian fare. The multicourse tasting menu can be paired with wines from the 2,500-bottle wine cellar. The dining experience is warm, with service that is attentive without being intimidating.

In 2007, the chef took a chance by opening Osteria a few blocks north of the business district in Center City. The antipasti, homemade pastas, authentic Neapolitan and Roman-style pizzas, and wood-fired meats drew diners as did the buzz of the classically designed, yet industrial space.

Vetri opened Amis Trattoria in Center City in 2010, and it was named one of the top ten places in the country for pasta by *Bon Appétit*. It got a sister at Philadelphia's Navy Yard when his Lo Spiedo was renamed Bar Amis in 2017. Vetri and crew then opened several locations of the casual Pizzeria Vetri, which serves wood-fired pizzas, craft beer, and wines on tap.

Left: Main dining room at Vetri Cucina. Photo courtesy of Vetri Family.
Right: Marc Vetri. Photo by Steve Legato.

Besides the restaurants, Vetri is well known for his philanthropic activities under the umbrella of the Vetri Community Partnership, which strives to help children and families experience the connection between healthy eating and healthy living in school cafeterias, after-school classes, and with a mobile teaching kitchen that goes into the neighborhoods.

In 2015, Urban Outfitters purchased Vetri's restaurants except for his namesake, Vetri Cucina. Two years later the chef stepped away from the restaurants operated by Urban Outfitters, staying involved only in Vetri Cucina and his charitable foundation. A few months later Chef Jeff Michaud, who helped Vetri open Osteria, bought it back from Urban Outfitters, with the backing of a local restaurateur.

Vetri Cucina
1312 Spruce St., 215-732-3478
vetricucina.com

Osteria
640 N. Broad St., 215-763-0920
osteriaphilly.com

Amis Trattoria/Bar Amis
412 S. 13th St. / 4503 S. Broad St.
215-732-2647 / 215-282-3184
amistrattoria.com

Pizzeria Vetri
1939 Callowhill St., 215-600-2629
1615 Chancellor St., 215-763-3760
640 W. DeKalb Pike King of Prussia, PA, 267-422-4201
pizzeriavetri.com

READING TERMINAL MARKET

125-year-old farmers market

The food-filled aisles of Reading Terminal Market, one of the nation's largest and oldest farmers' markets, are usually bustling with families, businesspeople, tourists, and conventioneers coming from the attached Pennsylvania Convention Center. It's a one-of-a-kind market with nearly one hundred kiosks including many owned by the same family for several generations and no chains. About forty percent of the kiosks sell prepared food, including a great ethnic mix from Pennsylvania Dutch to Greek and from soul food to a Jewish deli. You can also find Philadelphia delicacies, such as cheesesteaks, scrapple, hoagies, and freshly made pretzels. Other kiosks carry fresh produce, seafood, and meats at reasonable prices from longtime Philadelphia merchants, including Iovine Brothers Produce and Godshall's Poultry, which has been in the market since 1916.

For those who would like a "taste" of its history, the Taste of Philly Food Tour is highly recommended. Even locals will be fascinated by this food writer-created-and-led tour that tells the history of the vibrant market and its vendors, the stories behind Philadelphia foods, and includes several tastings. The seventy-five-minute walking tour weaves through the seventy-eight-thousand-square-foot market, which is set up like a small city, with wide avenues and narrower streets.

As you'll learn from tour leader Carolyn Wyman, in 1893, the Reading Railroad built a block-long terminal that had trains coming into the center of the city, combining the two existing farmers markets below into Reading Terminal Market. The fortune of the railroad, made immortal by Monopoly, ebbed and flowed, as did the market. The arrival of twelve Amish merchants in 1980 helped revive the market, and it hung in there for another decade until the

Left: Reading Terminal Market. Photo courtesy of Reading Terminal Market.

Right: Amish merchant at Reading Terminal Market. Photo courtesy of Reading Terminal Market.

Convention Center was built incorporating the former railroad terminal. It brought the market a much-needed renovation, an influx of new customers, and new vitality.

The most common meeting place at Reading Terminal used to be the antique clock at the corner of 12th and Market Streets, but now it's by Philbert, the 225-pound bronze pig in the seating area. For good luck, rub his snout, and to spread goodwill, feed him coins, which will be donated to charity.

Taste of Philly Food Tour
215-545-8007
phillyfunguide.com/tours/taste-of-philly-food-tour

Reading Terminal Market
51 N. 12th St., 215-922-2317
readingterminalmarket.org

Also see Bassetts Ice Cream (see page 24), Termini Bros. Bakery (see page 80) Mueller Chocolate (see page 3), Hershel's Deli (see page 46), Pretzels (see page 144), Metropolitan Bakery (see page 76), and Beiler's Doughnuts (see page 144).

If you can stand the heat

Once upon a time, diners avoided seats near the kitchen. Today, they're some of the most sought-after seats in the house. Many of Philadelphia's hippest restaurants have barstools that belly up to the open kitchen, providing a sneak peek for diners.

The kitchen counters provide a front-row seat as chefs prepare and plate salivation-worthy meals. Diners can feel the heat of the grill, smell the butter browning, see the pastry chef adding garnishes, and chat with the chef.

Some chefs attribute the popularity of the kitchen counter to the astronomical popularity of TV cooking shows and cooking classes. Cooking has become theater. They relish being in an open kitchen where they can actually watch guests enjoying their food and interact with them.

Diners can sometimes snag counter seats without reservations. Some of Philadelphia's most popular counters can be found at a.kitchen (see page 70), Amis Trattoria (see page 146), Suraya (see page 58), Audrey Claire, Barbuzzo Mediterranean Kitchen and Bar (see page 196), Jose Garces' Amada Philadelphia (see page 198), Michael Solomonov's Zahav and Abe Fisher (see page 48), Oloroso (see page 186), Hearthside, South (see page 88), Double Knot, Stephen Starr's Serpico with Chef Peter Serpico and his team (see page 200), and Vernick Food & Drink with Greg Vernick and his team (see page 72).

> **DON'T MISS:** No reservations? No counter seats? Check the bar. You can almost always get the full menu at the bar and you might just make a few new friends too.

Top: Counter seating at Amis Trattoria in Center City. Courtesy of Vetri Family.

Above left: Barbuzzo Interior. Photo by Jason Varney.

Above right: Audrey Claire. Photo by Irene Levy Baker.

Bottom: Chef Greg Vernick behind the counter at Vernick Food & Drink. Photo by Clay Williams.

RALPH'S ITALIAN RESTAURANT

America's oldest family-owned Italian restaurant

The Dispigno/Rubino family who own Ralph's Italian Restaurant isn't shy about putting the next generation to work. Ralph, whose father opened the restaurant in 1900, started to bus tables when he was just fifteen years old. His grandson, Jimmy Rubino, Jr., started even younger. When Jimmy was six years old, he was bussing tables in a little red velvet vest that matched the waiters' red vests. Maybe that's the kind of work ethic that it takes to keep a restaurant going for more than one hundred years.

In an industry where a ten-year run is considered successful, Ralph's has outlived not only every other Italian restaurant in the country but also the Great Depression, Prohibition, two World Wars, and nineteen presidents, including Theodore Roosevelt, who dined there. Other celebrities who have frequented the old-school Italian restaurant include Frank Sinatra, who would pat young Ralph on the head; Tony Bennett; Jack Klugman; former Vice President Joe Biden; Lidia Bastianich, who asked to put the restaurant's Chicken Tombino in one of her cookbooks; and Taylor Swift, who left a five hundred dollar tip.

It all started when Francesco Dispigno left Naples and headed to America with his wife, Catherine, and their young son, Rafael, whose name was later Americanized to Ralph. He opened a traditional Italian restaurant, commonly referred to in Philadelphia as a "red gravy" restaurant in the heart of the Italian Market in South Philadelphia. Fifteen years later they were able to expand into a boarding house just two blocks away.

Left: This mural of a classic Italian landscape has been on the wall since Ralph's opened, more than 115 years ago.

Right: Ralph's food.

When Francesco passed away in the 1930s, Ralph took over his namesake restaurant. Ralph and his wife, Mary, had four children who all worked in the restaurant. Their daughter Karen bought the house next door to the restaurant, and their daughter Elaine had two sons who became the fourth generation in the business. The grandsons, Jimmy Rubino, Jr. and Eddie, worked alongside Ralph, their grandfather, who came in daily until he was almost ninety years old. This fourth generation was responsible for restoring the original decor of the restaurant after an unfortunate redo in the 1970s and for parenting the fifth generation, who have started to follow their ancestors into the family business. Over the years, the restaurant has been passed down through five generations, along with the recipes brought over from the old country and still in use today.

760 S. 9th St., 215-627-6011

ralphsrestaurant.com

DON'T MISS: Any dish with red gravy (Philadelphia's term for homestyle tomato sauce). And be prepared for huge portions.

PHILADELPHIA'S CRAFT BREWERIES

What's brewing in Philadelphia

Philadelphia Founder William Penn had a brew house on his estate, Pennsbury Manor. George Washington was a home brewer, too, as was Thomas Jefferson, who said, "Beer, if drunk in moderation, softens the temper, cheers the spirit, and promotes health." Ben Franklin supposedly said, "Beer is proof that God loves us and wants us to be happy." While the origin of the quote is in dispute, Philadelphia's prominence in the brewing industry is not. In the 1800s, Philadelphia was a leader in beer production and considered the best beer brewing city outside of Europe. At its peak, seven hundred breweries could be found in the city, many in the area known, not surprisingly, as Brewerytown. That ebbed during Prohibition, but afterward beer was again flowing, and by the 1980s there was a new brewery boom.

Pennsylvanians love their beer. By 2016, 205 breweries in the Commonwealth were producing nearly four million barrels of craft beer per year, which was more barrels than anywhere else in the country according to the Brewers Association. That's 12.9 gallons per adult aged 21+, and the number of breweries keeps growing.

Today, the Philadelphia region has a wealth of craft breweries and brew pubs, including many marking their second decades—Victory, Yards, Flying Fish, Iron Hill, Sly Fox, and Philadelphia Brewing Company. All of these breweries offer tours. Smaller brewers, such as Saint Benjamin, Evil Genius, Free Will, and Forest & Main, have brewpubs and offer tours, and cult favorite, Tired Hands, has a brew cafe, fermentaria, and general store serving award-winning Belgian and French Farmhouse ales and American hop-forward ales.

Philly Beer Week held annually in June helped cement Philadelphia's reputation as a great beer town. It started in 2008 and

Left: Philadelphia Brewing Co. Photo by David Baker.
Right: Yards Brewing. Photo by Ben Lackey.

soon became a model for more than a hundred similar events around the world. Today, it is the largest beer celebration in America, with more than one thousand events at two hundred bars and breweries over ten days, including tastings of rare beers, a chance to meet brewers, massive parties, and a great excuse to have a hangover.

Thanks to the many award-winning brewers, Philly Beer Week, the amazing beer bars, and the charming beer gardens (see page 182), the city is regularly tapped for "best beer cities" lists, including *GQ*'s list of five best beer cities in America and *Frommer*'s list of Fourteen Best Beer Cities in the World.

Philadelphia Brewing Company
2440 Frankford Ave., 215-427-2739, philadelphiabrewing.com

Yards Brewing
500 Spring Garden St., 215-634-2600, yardsbrewing.com

Tired Hands Fermentaria
35 Cricket Terrace, Ardmore, PA, 484-413-2983, tiredhands.com

Tired Hands Brew Café
16 Ardmore Ave., Ardmore, PA, 610-896-7621

Tired Hands General Store
20 Ardmore Ave., Ardmore, PA, 484-413-2978

Philly Beer Week
phillylovesbeer.org

PHILADELPHIA CHEESESTEAKS

Chopped meat, wiz wit

The corner of 9th Street and East Passyunk, where Pat's King of Steaks and Geno's Steaks sit catty-corner from one another in the Italian Market, may be one of the most visited corners in Philadelphia. With its neon on steroids and limousines pulling up with wedding parties and celebrities, such as Oprah Winfrey, Justin Timberlake, presidents, and political candidates, it's certainly a notable corner and worth a visit. Go with a friend, get a cheesesteak at both places, then swap halves, so you can choose your favorite. For an authentic cheesesteak, order it "wiz wit." That's with Cheez Whiz, not provolone, and with grilled onions, atop thinly grilled steak on a fresh roll.

Every local has a favorite steak place. Ask around and you'll often hear John's Roast Pork (where you'll also want to try the iconic roast pork sandwich), Jim's Steaks, or Tony Luke's.

Philadelphia's love affair with steak sandwiches was started in 1930 by Pat Olivieri, a hot dog vendor. Undoubtedly tired of eating hot dogs for lunch every day, Olivieri grilled up some chopped meat and onions for himself and put them on a hot dog roll. A passing cab driver, who was a regular at the hot dog cart, asked to try one and then convinced Olivieri to sell the steak sandwich instead of hot dogs.

DON'T MISS: Geno's Gear, a Geno's-themed gift shop across the street from the cheesesteak stand.

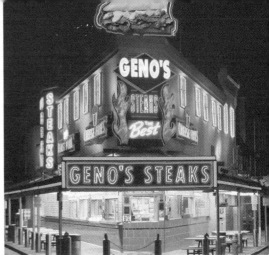

Top left: Pat's Exterior. Photo by Pravada Photography.

Top right: Geno's exterior. Photo courtesy of Geno's.

Above left: Frank Olivieri, Pat's great nephew, at Pat's King of Steaks. Photo by Pravada Photography.

Above right: Geno Vento, who was named after the cheesesteak shop his father, Joey Vento, opened in 1966.

Now, nearly a century later, this makeshift lunch is an icon of Philadelphia that can be found on menus across the country.

Pat's King of Steaks
1237 E. Passyunk Ave., 215-468-1546, patskingofsteaks.com

Geno's Steaks
1219 S. 9th St., 215-389-0659, genosteaks.com

PHILADELPHIA DISTILLERIES

Fatherly fermentation

Philadelphia is not just a craft beer town. With more than a dozen in the region, it's also becoming a hub for distilleries. Distilling began to flourish in 2011 when the Commonwealth of Pennsylvania passed reforms that enabled distillers to offer tours and tastings on-site.

The fathers of three local distillers each played an important role in their sons' distilleries—Mountain Laurel Spirits, Federal Distilling, and Five Saints Distilling.

Herman C. Mihalich, who cofounded Mountain Laurel Spirits, named his Rye Whiskey after his dad, calling it Dad's Hat Pennsylvania Rye Whiskey. His dad had a wardrobe of hats and each day picked the one that fit the occasion or his mood. To his son, the fashion statement was also an unspoken commitment to quality, polish, and finish. Mihalich and John S. Cooper, his cofounder and college buddy, were seeking the same qualities in their rye whiskey. Mihalich kept his father's hat collection and wears the hats—like the name, they're a perfect fit.

Bryan and Matthew Quigley started distilling vodka in an unused corner of their parents' basement. When their father discovered their pastime, he made it clear that their family home was not to be used as a distillery. Though the enterprising brothers lost their subterranean production facility, they didn't give up. They learned the business, got tastings into the right mouths, and found investors. Federal Distilling's signature product, Stateside Urbancraft Vodka, is now made not in a basement but in a South Kensington facility with an attached cocktail lounge.

John Robert George named his distillery Five Saints after his father, three uncles, and a close friend, who served as father figures after his father's untimely passing. The men, who George thinks

Left: Herman Mihalich, founder and distiller, Mountain Laurel Spirits.

Right: John G. George, one of the namesakes of Five Saints Distilling, with sons, John R. (left) owner of the distillery and Randy, circa 1960.

of as "saints" for their patient guidance during his upbringing, are honored with portraits above the bar. The Norristown-based microdistillery currently makes award-winning vodka, white whiskey, gin, and blood-orange liqueur and cocktails. The distillery is housed in a firehouse dating back to 1888. Like the fathers he honors, Five Saints is committed to family, community, and quality.

The three father-influenced distilleries are part of the Philadelphia Distillery Tours, a group of eleven distilleries that have banded together to promote the industry and encourage people to explore and taste the handcrafted spirits being made in the region.

Federal Distilling

1700 N. Hancock St., 215-425-4200

statesidevodka.com

Five Saints Distilling

129 E. Main St., Norristown, PA, 610-279-5364

fivesaintsdistilling.com

Mountain Laurel Spirits

925 Canal St., Building #4, Door 16, Bristol, PA, 215-781-8300

dadshatrye.com

Philadelphia Distillery Tours

phillydistillerytrail.com

Trading in suits for boots

Deb Lutz got her education at some of the country's finest schools and then took a traditional business route marketing consumer packaged goods, food and beverages, and over-the-counter medication. She rose to the top ranks of a multinational consumer goods company, but it left her unfulfilled.

After more than two decades on the fast track in corporate America, Lutz was ready for a change. She wanted to do something on her own that she could feel good about. As a mom of two children (including one on a restrictive diet), she was always struggling with fast meal options that worked for her family.

When Lutz heard about b.good, she knew she had found her new direction. The healthier fast-casual restaurant was started in 2003 by two boyhood friends and quickly became popular in New England. B.good has a locally sourced and seasonally inspired menu, including house-ground burgers, homemade vegetable burgers, handcut fries, salads, smoothies, and shakes.

Lutz has seen the power of family meals in her own home. Her teenage daughter was diagnosed with Prader-Willi syndrome when she was just a baby. This rare genetic disorder leads to developmental delays, including feeding difficulties, an insatiable appetite, and chronic overeating. By necessity, Lutz's home has a strong focus on food and eating habits, which is one more reason that b.good's mission and menu caught her eye.

She fell in love with the concept and opened its first Philadelphia area location in Marlton, New Jersey. Then she opened locations in King of Prussia, Pennsylvania, and Mt. Laurel, New Jersey. She has plans to open several more. Lutz is the only female franchisee.

These days it's not unusual to find Lutz donning boots and tramping

Left: Deb Lutz.

Right: Dining at b.good. Photo courtesy of b.good.

around area farms to find locally grown ingredients. Milk and ice cream are sourced from grass-fed cows at Trickling Springs Creamery in Chambersburg, Pennsylvania; cheeses from Lancaster, Pennsylvania; and produce from farms in Salem, Hammonton, and Vineland, New Jersey.

When Lutz traded in her suits for boots, she found the fulfillment she was seeking.

Town Center, 150 Main St. Suite 160, King of Prussia, PA, 484-322-2110
Centerton Shopping Center, 26 Centerton Rd., Mount Laurel, NJ, 856-242-3717
The Promenade at Sagemore, 500 Route 73 South, Marlton, NJ, 856-988-0275
facebook.com/bgoodphilly

THE OLDE BAR

Pays homage to Bookbinders

Bookbinders was once one of the most chichi restaurants in Philadelphia. The nationally known seafood restaurant was a magnet for celebrities, big spenders, and those celebrating special occasions, but it slowly declined over the years and eventually closed its doors. After many years of sitting empty, some of the old sparkle returned in 2015 when a celebrity chef reopened it.

It all started in 1893 when Samuel Bookbinder opened a modest oyster saloon on Fifth Street near South Street. Five years later he moved it to Second Street at Walnut Street. Called Old Original Bookbinders, the restaurant was a real step up. It was known for its opulence, massive lobster tank, snapper soup, private dining room modeled after the room where the Declaration of Independence was signed, and for attracting the patronage of celebrities, including Babe Ruth, Tennessee Williams, Teddy Roosevelt, Al Jolson, Elizabeth Taylor, and Frank Sinatra.

After its heyday, the restaurant was willed to charity but made a comeback in 1945 when John Taxin bought it. He ran it with his son, Albert, and it eventually fell into the hands of his grandson and sister before closing in 2002. A downsized version opened in 2005 but was short-lived.

Meanwhile, after a family quarrel, two of Samuel's grandsons opened Bookbinder's 15th Street Seafood House in 1935. That restaurant, on 15th Street, was run by the family for four generations until it closed in 2003. The two restaurants had a friendly rivalry. By 2007, both iconic Philadelphia restaurants were closed.

Top right: Shucker at The Olde Bar.

Above left: Old Original Bookbinders.

Above right: The Olde Bar.

Then the space sat idle for many years before a new restaurant opened with a tip of its hat to the previous tenant. In 2015, Chef Jose Garces (see page 198), a prolific Philadelphia restaurateur, opened The Olde Bar in the Old Original Bookbinder's space. Garces' restaurant is a contemporary oyster bar, cocktail lounge, and event space that pays homage to the original.

125 Walnut St., 215-253-3777

theoldebar.com

DON'T MISS: The Olde Bar participates in the Delaware Estuary Oyster Shell Recycling Program, which returns shells to the Delaware Bay allowing baby oysters to grow.

WM. MULHERIN'S SONS

Making a name for itself

William J. Mulherin emigrated from Ireland to the United States in 1848. Two and a half decades later he opened a whiskey blending and bottling business, calling it William J. Mulherin. In 1899, the name changed to Wm. Mulherin & Sons for obvious reasons, and shortly thereafter the business moved into a three-story building at Front and Master Streets in the heart of Fishtown. After William's death in 1913, his sons changed the name of the business to Wm. Mulherin's Sons and had the new name carved into the stonework of their imposing building. The whiskey business lasted another decade, closing in 1924, largely due to Prohibition.

The building then sat empty for close to one hundred years until restoration began in 2014. Great care was taken to maintain the industrial character, history, and decor of the building, including the terra cotta exterior signs, arched windows, vestibule, interior millwork, and safe. It was the same respect for history that motivated the restaurant to preserve the original name that's carved into the building—Wm. Mulherin's Sons.

Wm. Mulherin's Sons calls itself a neighborhood joint, but it's attracting patrons as well as media attention from far and

> **DON'T MISS:** The industrial-cool four-room hotel above the restaurant, also called Wm. Mulherin's Sons, offers such amenities as a growler program that can provide libations for guests to enjoy in their room, a cocktail kit, and a coffee program curated by La Colombe, a nearby coffee roaster (see page 142). Guests check in with the restaurant staff below, just as at a classic English pub.

Top right: Wm. Mulherin's Sons Hotel exterior at Front Street. Photo by Matthew Williams.

Above left: Wm. Mulherin's Sons bar corner booth. Photo by Matthew Williams.

Above right: Wm. Mulherin's Sons dining room and concrete fireplace. Photo by Matthew Williams.

wide, including *Bon Appétit*, which named it to the list of Best Restaurants in America when it opened in 2016. The restaurant specializes in wood-fired small plates, pizza, and pasta, drawing out the smokiness and char imparted by the wood-burning oven and grill.

Fittingly for a bar in a former nineteenth century whiskey blending and bottling factory, Wm. Mulherin's Sons has an intriguing list of expertly prepared cocktails as well as craft beer and wines.

A healthy respect for history helped the restaurant find its name, as it makes a name for itself in the nation's restaurant scene.

1355 N. Front St., 215-291-1355

wmmulherinssons.com

RIVAL BROS. COFFEE ROASTERS

From cocktail napkin to truck to coffee bars

Late at night after the restaurant where they worked closed Jonathan Adams and Damien Pileggi could often be found huddled together in a local bar sketching ideas on cocktail napkins and talking about the future. Adams and Pileggi grew up together just outside of Philadelphia in Bucks County, later became roommates, and then worked together at restaurants.

Adams eventually pursued a career as a chef, and Pileggi, who had developed a passion for coffee while working at La Colombe (see page 142), left for the West Coast to study coffee roasting and brewing. When Pileggi returned to Philadelphia, he was ready to apply what he'd learned, and the two dug out those old cocktail napkins.

In 2011, after the pair had spent time perfecting their roasts, they officially launched Rival Bros. Coffee from their mobile cafe, a retrofitted delivery truck. Although they don't really consider themselves rivals, they liked the playful twist on their longtime friendship so they created a logo showing a boxing match and gave their roasts boxing-related names, such as Palooka and Featherweight. The food truck provided a great way for Adams and Pileggi to test their concept and build a following with lower overhead than a brick-and-mortar coffee bar. Like other successful food trucks, including Mac Mart (see page 174) and Revolution Taco, it wasn't long before Rival Bros. had a big enough following to expand.

In spring 2014, Adams and Pileggi retired their mobile cafe to focus their efforts on opening their first brick-and-mortar coffee bar,

Left: Jonathan Adams and Damien Pileggi at the Rittenhouse location. Photo by Jason Varney.
Right: Tasker location. Photo by Jason Varney.

located in the city's Fitler Square neighborhood, attracting a mix of professionals, students, and artists. In spring 2017, they followed up with their second coffee bar in a large majestic space with high ceilings in the Touraine Building in the Rittenhouse Square area, and the third opened in fall of the same year along East Passyunk in South Philadelphia. At each location, they serve a selection of drip coffee and espresso beverages from their proprietary line of beans, which is roasted daily at their facility in the city's Frankford section, as well as twelve-ounce bags of their freshly roasted coffee. Additional beverages, ranging from draft cold-brew and nitro-brewed coffee to loose-leaf teas to all-natural sodas, are also available throughout the day, as well as snacks from other small local food businesses.

2400 Lombard St.
1528 Spruce St.
1100 Tasker St.
rivalbros.com

Mushroom Capital of the World

Kennett Square is home to about sixty-five small, family-owned mushroom farms that produce more than one million pounds of mushrooms a week, earning it the moniker of mushroom capital of the world. Those farms, many of which have been in the same family for four generations, supply about half the country's mushrooms.

Why is there a concentration of mushroom farmers in this cozy hamlet about an hour from Center City Philadelphia? It started in 1885, when two Quaker florists found that mushrooms grew well in the cool, dark, damp spaces below their carnations in the basement of their facility on Willow Street. The mushroom business grew like wild flowers, and by 1896, they opened the first building in the area dedicated to growing mushrooms. Several factors make Kennett Square ideal for mushroom growing: the composition of the soil, the cooperative nature of the Quaker farmers who shared innovations, a large population of Italian immigrants to work on the farms, and the availability of good transportation systems providing easy access to raw materials and proximity to markets to get the perishable products distributed quickly.

Kennett Square-based Phillips Mushroom Farms is the largest grower of specialty mushrooms in the United States. Every year it ships thirty-five million pounds of mushrooms from its four farms in Pennsylvania and one in Maryland. William Phillips started with a small mushroom farm in 1926. Forty years later his sons, R. Marshall and Donald, formed a partnership and expanded the business.

DON'T MISS: Kennett Square's The Mushroom Cap, a mushroom-centric boutique, and La Michoacana, home of such ice cream flavors as avocado and rice pudding.

Left: William's sons, Donald and Marshall Phillips.

Right: Mushrooms at The Woodlands at Phillips.

Today, two of Donald's three sons run the farm, and Marshall's three daughters handle The Woodlands at Phillips, a retail store and museum. Some of the brothers and sisters-in-law married into both the family and the business, and a fourth generation is not far behind.

While the indoor mushroom farms are off-limits, foodies can visit The Woodlands at Phillips, where there's a small but interesting free museum with a mushroom-growing exhibit, displays about the farm's 90+ year mushroom-growing history, and videos about growing mushrooms. There's also a restored farmhouse with a mushroom-centric store selling gifts, gourmet foods, fresh Phillips mushrooms, and hosting cooking demonstrations by local chefs.

The community celebrates its bounty with two annual mushroom events— Midnight in the Square on New Year's Eve (a giant mushroom drop) and the Mushroom Festival held the weekend after Labor Day.

The Woodlands at Phillips
1020 Kaolin Rd., Kennett Square, PA, 610-444-2192, thewoodlandsatphillips.com

The Mushroom Cap
114 W. State St., Kennett Square, PA, 610-444-8484, themushroomcap.com

La Michoacana
231 E. State St., Kennett Square, PA, 610-444-2996
facebook.com/la-michoacana-homemade-ice-cream

REVOLUTIONARY HOSPITALITY

A role in the American Revolution

If the walls at Black Powder Tavern could talk, they would reveal the secrets that General George Washington shared with the Marquis de Lafayette at clandestine meetings during the Revolutionary War. Legend has it that leaders of the Continental Army met, strategized, and perhaps even threw back a few beers there. It is said that during the infamous winter of 1777–1778 when Continental soldiers were holed up just a few miles away at Valley Forge, Friedrich von Steuben used the site as a secret stash for black powder munitions. The tavern has been serving food, beer, and revolutionary hospitality since 1746.

White Horse Tavern was another popular meeting place during the American Revolution. The original White Horse Tavern, built in 1715, was one of the first licensed public houses in America. It served as a way station for colonists on the road west, including revolutionaries and loyalists of all classes. In 1777, after losing the grueling eleven-hour Battle of Brandywine, General George Washington regrouped at the tavern. It was an ideal location, as it provided a view of the valley and hills to the south and access to escape routes. When Washington withdrew, Hessian soldiers moved in, robbing the proprietor, John Kerlin, of 199 pounds. Today, the Tavern, which is part of the Sheraton Great Valley Hotel, serves traditional American cuisine with a classic Colonial ambiance.

The building that houses Savona Restaurant, a Main Line staple since 1997, was constructed in the 1760s and served as headquarters for Aaron Burr during the Revolutionary War. Burr became the third vice president of the United States under Thomas Jefferson and later shot his rival, Alexander Hamilton, in a duel.

Left: General Warren. Photo courtesy of the General Warren.

Right: Black Powder Tavern. Photo by David Baker.

The Admiral Vernon Inne opened in 1745. In 1758, it was renamed the Admiral Warren Inn after Admiral Peter Warren, who defended the American colonies during the French and Indian War. At that time, it was owned by William Penn's grandson, John Penn, who was a loyalist, and the building served as a Tory stronghold. Loyalists met, drew maps, plotted the Paoli Massacre, and possibly even tortured the local blacksmith there. They might be surprised to find that their old haunt was again renamed to make amends with the new nation. It is now a fine dining establishment and bed and breakfast called the General Warren.

Black Powder Tavern
1164 Valley Forge Rd., Wayne, PA, 610-293-9333
blackpowdertavern.com

White Horse Tavern
707 E. Lancaster Ave., Frazer, PA, 610-280-2095
whitehorsetavernandwinebar.com

Savona
100 Old Gulph Rd., Gulph Mills, PA, 610-520-1200
savonarestaurant.com

General Warren
9 Old Lancaster Rd., Malvern, PA, 610-296-3637
generalwarren.com

FANTE'S KITCHEN SHOP

The oldest cookware store in the U.S.

Fante's, the oldest cookware store in the country, has been serving the Philadelphia community for more than one hundred years. Fante's carries a dozen different types of pizzelle makers, a solid brass duck press, more than one hundred cookie cutter shapes, and three dozen different kinds of rolling pins as well as everyday kitchen equipment and even a coffee bar. Not only locals love to lose themselves in the winding, seemingly endless aisles but also chefs, cookbook authors, Food TV hosts, and other celebrities, including Julia Child, Mario Batali, Lidia Bastianich, Martin Yan, Mary Ann Esposito, Rose Levy Beranbaum, Nathalie Dupree, Emeril Lagasse, Stanley Tucci, Patti LaBelle, and James Darren. Shoppers will feel like kids in a candy store. The attraction isn't only the plethora of fun, interesting, and unusual products but also the personal service shoppers receive at this family-owned and run store.

Italian immigrants Domenico Fante and his son, Luigi, opened the store in 1906 in the heart of the Italian Market (see page 98). After they passed, Luigi's son, Dominic, continued the family tradition. The third-generation owner was known for helping new immigrants settle into the neighborhood and working to protect their rights. By 1981, when the Fantes were ready to retire, they turned the business over to Mariella Giovannucci Esposito, their longtime manager and protege who had started working there when she was a seventeen-year-old Italian immigrant who would speak to customers in her native Italian. Mariella and her brothers, Nick and Daniele Giovannucci, her sister, Eugenia Dantz, and her daughter, Liana

Top: Pizzelle makers at Fante's. Photo by Irene Levy Baker.

Above left: Mariella Esposito with Michael Solomonov and Steven Cook of CookNSolo Restaurants. (see page 48)

Above right: Luigi and Carmela Fante, with children Rose, Teresa, Frank, Dominic and Josephine, circa 1912.

Esposito Ottaviani, still run the store today along with about a dozen employees who are like family and mostly live in the neighborhood.

1006 S. 9th St., 215-922-5557

fantes.com

Philadelphia's first mac and cheesery

When Marti Lieberman graduated from Drexel University, her mother threw her a lovely graduation party. With a menu of healthy, grown-up food her mother had carefully chosen from a local caterer, Lieberman knew it would be a … disaster. College kids don't want to eat broccoli salad, deli meats, and tuna fish sandwiches. She hastily ran to the grocery store, loaded up her cart with the junk foods college students crave—think guacamole and chips and cupcakes—and then rushed home and made a pan of macaroni and cheese. It was a big, gooey hit!

Little did Lieberman or her mother know that this episode foreshadowed her future career as Philadelphia's contessa of mac and cheese. First, the new college graduate followed her lifelong dream and got a job in the fashion world. After three months, she knew fashion wasn't a good fit for her. She also noticed that her coworkers loved the pans of mac and cheese that she often brought for parties. Her friends were asking for it too.

Lieberman decided to trade her high-fashion suits for food-stained sweats, and she began making her mac and cheese full-time. Her mother was skeptical, but Lieberman felt confident that she could fashion a successful business from the classic American comfort food. She got a food truck, painted it bright pink so that it would stand out, and hit the road. Her boyfriend, Garrett, and her sister, Pamela, jumped in to help.

The pink truck debuted on the Drexel campus in 2013, and it wasn't long before thrillist.com named it one of the ten best food trucks in Philadelphia. As Lieberman demonstrated at her college graduation party, people were really eating up the creamy mac and cheese made with seven cheeses and topped with a crunchy panko and potato topping.

Top: Mac Mart truck

Above left: Mac Mart food. Photo courtesy of MacMart.

Above right: Sisters Pamela (left) and Marti Lieberman.

By 2016, Leiberman was successful enough to open her first location and expand her menu to include custom mix-ins ranging from bacon to barbecue chicken chunks, fried or caramelized onions, roasted red peppers, spinach and artichoke dip, and even jumbo lump crabmeat and Old Bay potato chips.

Besides the students, business executives, residents, and visitors who line up to order Leiberman's mac and cheese, her mother is now Mac Mart's biggest fan, and perhaps the proudest too.

104 S. 18th St., 215-444-6144

macmartcart.com

WOK'N WALK TOURS OF CHINATOWN

Showcasing the history, culture, and foods of Chinatown

The story of Chef Joseph Poon's career could be the script of a Hollywood movie. Poon's training began when he was a teenager working in airline food service in Hong Kong. The chef's carved fruit and vegetable centerpieces and sculptures fascinated him. When the chef refused Poon's request for a lesson, Poon purchased several hundred potatoes and practiced until he mastered the skill. The art became one of his trademarks. Poon showed that same tenacity when he arrived in Philadelphia with eight dollars in his pocket and a limited knowledge of English. He worked as a dishwasher and then as a waiter, in construction, and in a fortune cookie factory, holding as many as three jobs at a time.

Poon became known for Joe's Peking Duck House and his Asian fusion restaurants (all now closed) in Philadelphia's Chinatown (see page 90), his commitment to philanthropy, his Wok'N Walk Tours of Chinatown, and his elaborate vegetable carving.

Poon conducts his Chinatown tour for private groups of twenty or more. The popular walking tour was called one of the best culinary tours in the country by TV's Food Network. It provides an insider's look at one of Philadelphia's most vibrant ethnic communities, including stops at a Chinese herb store, an Asian bakery to taste bubble tea, a Buddhist Temple, an Asian grocery store and fish market. A Chinese vegetable carving lesson and meal with Chef Poon at a Chinatown restaurant can be included as well.

Chef Joseph Poon in front of Philadelphia's Chinese Friendship Gate.

Poon's warmth and exuberance have kept national TV audiences entertained and earned him appearances on *The Tonight Show* with Jay Leno and *The Ellen DeGeneres Show*. A half-page personality profile in *The New York Times* said, "In the last three decades, Mr. Poon has risen from impoverished immigrant to national culinary fame, known for his Asian fusion fare, his ability to carve bulbous watermelons and pumpkins into delicate swans, and his role in opening the center of the region's Asian community to the outside world."

When he is not conducting tours, Poon travels around the United States and Canada doing vegetable carving demonstrations for the National Watermelon Promotion Board, growers, farmers, and others. He also travels the world on a never-ending quest for more culinary knowledge.

215-500-9774

josephpoon.com

FERRY MARKET

New Hope's newest addition

The Ferry Market in New Hope has become a hub of community activity with indoor and outdoor seating and more than a dozen vendors, each with a locally-made product and a story to tell, including a couple who stumbled upon a previously unknown talent that changed the direction of their lives.

Every year, Tom and Loren Sciascia, graphic designers, gave their clients lovely holiday gifts. Then, during the holiday season right after 9/11, the couple really wanted to give their clients holiday gifts that were warmer, more personal and from the heart. That year, rather than giving store bought gifts, Tom cracked open one of his hundreds of dessert cookbooks and made chocolate truffles. The clients liked the truffles so much that they ordered more truffles to give out as their holiday gifts. Eventually, the couple left graphic design and put their creative talents into the fine art of chocolate and Sciascia Confections was born. They hand-craft more than thirty kinds of chocolate truffles, chocolate bars, barks, brownies, authentic French macarons in a rainbow of colors, and to-die-for hot drinking chocolate. Though their business has changed, the desire to treat each customer with warmth and personal service remains strong for this husband-wife duo.

The Ferry Market is a good fit for New Hope, a picturesque town in Bucks County. *Travel & Leisure* named New Hope, which has a strong gay community, one of the coolest suburbs in the country. It

> **DON'T MISS:** The French macarons at Sciascia Confections. The freshly-made gems just might beat the ones you taste in Paris. Look for flavors like salted caramel cheesecake, red velvet and birthday cake with vanilla bean buttercream.

Left: Macarons. Photo courtesy of Sciascia Confections.

Right: Chocolates from Sciascia Confections. Photo courtesy of Sciascia Confections.

is full of quirky independently-owned shops, galleries, and unique restaurants like Marsha Brown, a Creole restaurant in a renovated church and Logan Inn, which is so old that General George Washington dined there.

Sherri and Kevin Daugherty, the owners of the Ferry Market, are wonderful friends to New Hope. Over the years, the couple has worked tirelessly to enhance the community by providing funding for Bucks County Playhouse (which opened in 1939 and launched Grace Kelly and Robert Redford) and developing the Carriage House and the Playhouse Inn. The charming hamlet just keeps getting better and better.

Ferry Market

32 South Main St. New Hope, PA, 609-240-5983

theferrymarket.com

Sciascia Confections

Ferry Market, 32 South Main St., New Hope, PA

Stockton Market, 19 Bridge St., Stockton, NJ

215-996-0606

sciasciaconfections.com

PHILADELPHIA RESTAURANT WEEK

Get a taste of the Philadelphia restaurant scene

The most affordable time to get a taste of Philadelphia's restaurant scene is during Restaurant Week when more than a hundred restaurants offer three-course dinners for thirty-five dollars. Many also offer a twenty dollar lunch menu. The much anticipated event typically takes place in January and again in September and lasts twelve days. Although Restaurant Week does not officially include Saturday night, many restaurants offer their Restaurant Week menu on the Saturday that falls in the middle of the event.

Restaurant Week was created by Center City District in 2003 as an economic driver for restaurants during what are often slow seasons. It's been so successful in Philadelphia that it has spawned similar events in the surrounding neighborhoods and suburbs.

Many restaurants are sold out during Restaurant Week, so be sure to make reservations. Some restaurants only serve the prix fixe menu, while others offer their regular a la carte menu as well. The price for the prix fixe does not include alcohol, tax, or gratuity.

DON'T MISS: If you're driving into the city, check Center City District's website (CenterCityPhila.org) for parking and ride share discounts during Philadelphia Restaurant Week.

Top right: Diners at Scarpetta during Restaurant Week. Photo by Steve Legato. Courtesy of Center City District.

Above left: Restaurant Week dishes at SUGA. Photo by Steve Legato. Courtesy of Center City District.

Above right: Dilworth Plaza during Center City Sips. Photo by Matt Stanley. Courtesy of Center City District.

Center City District is also the mastermind behind Center City Sips, which is held on Wednesday evenings from 5:00 p.m. to 7:00 p.m. throughout the summer. Nearly one hundred bars and restaurants offer discounted beer, wine, cocktails, and appetizers.

215-440-5500
CenterCityPhila.org

Great brews and views

The proliferation of beer gardens around the city has helped boost its cool factor significantly. While some are year-round hangouts, many are seasonal, including Spruce Street Harbor Park, Independence Beer Garden, and Bok Bar.

Spruce Street Harbor Park, along the Delaware River waterfront, has become a must-see warm weather destination. *The Huffington Post* called it one of the "best urban beaches in the world." It's an urban oasis with striped hammocks and cozy seating, fountains, floating barges with food and drink kiosks, and oversized games illuminated by hundreds of hanging color-changing lights.

Independence Beer Garden provides not only great views of Independence National Historical Park but also forty craft beers. Relax at picnic tables or in Adirondack chairs or challenge someone to ping pong or a board game. Small seating areas and ivy-covered pergolas make the twenty-thousand-square-foot space feel surprisingly intimate.

Edward W. Bok Technical High School, a public technical high school that closed in 2013, didn't stray too far from its roots when it was transformed into a work space for artists, small businesses, nonprofits, and small-batch manufacturers. But the former students probably couldn't have imagined its hip rooftop bar with breathtaking views of the city skyline in their wildest dreams. Be forewarned. You won't see the river-to-river views without an ID, even if you're old enough to have children over the age of twenty-one.

Two more places with great brews and views: The Skyline Terrace at the main branch of the Free Library of Philadelphia on the Ben Franklin Parkway and Balcony Bar on the outdoor terrace at the Kimmel Center for the Performing Arts on the Avenue of the Arts. Plus, every season the Pennsylvania Horticultural Society transforms

Left: Independence Beer Garden restaurant dining. Photo by Irene Levy Baker.

Right: Spruce Street Harbor Park. Photo by Matt Stanley.

a few underused lots into imaginative and inviting beer gardens, and the Parks on Tap program creates roving beer gardens by bringing food and drink trucks to twenty city parks over the course of twenty weeks, thanks to Fairmount Park Conservancy, Philadelphia Parks & Recreation, and FCM Hospitality.

The flourishing microbreweries in the area and the many awesome places to drink brews are cementing Philadelphia's standing as one of the best beer cities in the country.

Spruce St. Harbor Park
Columbus Blvd. and Spruce St., 215-922-2386, delawareriverwaterfront.com

Independence Beer Garden
100 S. Independence Mall West, 215-922-7100, phlbeergarden.com

Bok Bar
800 Mifflin St., 215-220-6815, bok-bar.com

Skyline Terrace at the Free Library of Philadelphia
1901 Vine St. at the Benjamin Franklin Parkway, 215-686-5322, freelibrary.org

Kimmel Center for the Performing Arts
300 S. Broad St., 215-790-5800, kimmelcenter.org

Parks on Tap
215-568-1616, parksontap.com

Pennsylvania Horticultural Society
215-988-8800, phsonline.org

Beloved convenience store

Nearly every Philadelphian has a story about Wawa, and many are downright obsessed with it. The more than fifty-year-old chain of convenience stores inspires flash mobs, tattoos, and soliloquies by rabid fans who buy more than 195 million cups of Wawa coffee and eighty million hoagies a year.

Wawa has more than 760 stores in Pennsylvania, New Jersey, Delaware, Maryland, Virginia, and Florida. Each store sells about six thousand items, including coffee and Wawa's own brands of dairy products and iced tea, juice, and other cold drinks. It's also the largest purveyor of freshly made sandwiches and hoagies in the Delaware Valley. Wawa was an early adopter of touch screen computer ordering and provides a reliably quick, inexpensive meal that's better than a fast-food restaurant. It's open twenty-four hours a day/365 days a year. What's not to love?

The beloved convenience store is named for Wawa, Pennsylvania, a small town about twenty-five miles west of Philadelphia. "Wawa," a Native American word for Canadian Goose, also inspired the company's logo. The company encourages employees, who benefit from an employee stock ownership plan, to create "goose bump moments"—the stuff that legends are made of—for customers.

The legend started in 1902 when George Wood opened a small dairy farm in Wawa, Pennsylvania, where he processed and then delivered milk. Today, Wawa still operates a dairy that sells more

DON'T MISS: Wawa's secret menu. It's revealed when you click the flying goose in the bottom left corner of the main ordering screen then hit "enter here."

Top left: Wawa dairy.

Top right: Wawa associates.

Above left: Wawa store interior.

Above right: Wawa products.

than ninety-two million quarts of milk annually, but thanks to George's grandson, Grahame Wood, who realized that shopping habits were changing, in 1964 it entered the convenience store business too. It remains privately held, and all stores are company owned and operated.

Wawa was instrumental in getting hoagies named the "official sandwich of Philadelphia" and is a title sponsor of the Wawa Welcome America Festival, the city's annual 4th of July Festival, further cementing the devotion of Philadelphians and fans living elsewhere who tend to bond over their longing for their hometown c-store.

wawa.com

Culinary chemist found formula for success

Townsend Wentz studied organic chemistry at Rutgers University. By day, Wentz attended classes; by night, he worked in restaurants to support himself. Once he graduated, Wentz worked as a food scientist and began studying for an additional degree in biology. He continued to moonlight in restaurant kitchens to pay off his student loans.

Both jobs were methodical, but his day job felt slow and tedious, while the restaurant work felt fast-paced and exhilarating. On a fluke, he accepted a one-day stage (unpaid internship) at what was then the Four Seasons, Philadelphia, where the Fountain Restaurant was run by Philadelphia culinary legend Jean-Marie LaCroix.

That motivated him to spend years honing his skills at restaurants throughout Philadelphia. In 2014, Wentz opened Townsend, a seasonal French restaurant that sits in a two-floor row house on East Passyunk Avenue. The culinary chemist clearly had the formula for success, since shortly after opening, his eponymous restaurant was named to Zagat's list of the 12 Hottest French Restaurants in America and *Bon Appétit*'s List of America's Best New Restaurants. Additional accolades followed.

Two years later Wentz opened A Mano, a cozy Italian BYOB in Fairmount. A Mano means "by hand" and may refer to how the cuisine is prepared, but it could also refer to the painstaking renovation in which Wentz played a hands-on role. In the fall of 2017, he opened Oloroso, a Spanish tapas restaurant in Washington Square West.

Top right: Bar at Oloroso. Photo by James Zeleniak/PUNCH Media.

Above left: Townsend exterior. Photo by Neal Santos.

Above right: Chef Townsend Wentz at Oloroso. Photo by James Zeleniak/PUNCH Media.

Townsend
1623 E. Passyunk Ave., 267-639-3203
townsendrestaurant.com

A Mano
2244 Fairmount Ave., 215-236-1114
amanophilly.com

Oloroso
1121 Walnut St., 267-324-3014
olorosophilly.com

DON'T MISS: Valet parking. On Friday and Saturday nights, you'll find valet parking at the Singing Fountain in East Passyunk Square.

The cuisine of Taiwan

When Judy Ni first told her parents she was interested in pursuing a career in the restaurant business, they could not hide their disappointment. Judy's mother, who holds degrees in food science and computer science, and her father, a Ph.D. in chemical engineering, didn't envision their daughter living the difficult life of a restaurateur and tried to dissuade her.

Ni was originally on the more traditional path her parents envisioned, attending college and working in finance, followed by a few years at a company that produced products sold at major retailers.

But Ni wasn't content, and, despite her parents' objections, decided to pursue a restaurant job. Ni first observed the restaurant industry from a family friend's Chinese-American restaurant, which, to her parents' chagrin, only further motivated her to join the industry. After numerous calls to restaurants offering to wash dishes and serve as free labor, she landed a kitchen job in northern New Jersey. Afterward, to round out her experience, she took a front-of-the-house job at New Jersey's Montville Inn, where she met her future husband and business partner, Andy Tessier.

Next, the couple began a multiyear journey in fine dining. Tessier worked for Chef Daniel Boulud's restaurants in New York City, and Ni went to Blue Hill at Stone Barns in New York's Hudson Valley. Eventually, they settled in Philadelphia, where they worked at Josh Lawler's now-closed The Farm & Fisherman while sussing out the market for the potential of opening the bāo • logy concept.

Left: bāo • logy wonton soup. Photo courtesy of bāo • logy.

Right: bāo • logy interior. Photo courtesy of bāo • logy.

They opened their fast-casual Taiwanese restaurant, bāo • logy, in 2017. Ni's business acumen, coupled with her restaurant experience and engaging personality, makes her a force to be reckoned with. Her charm is evident as she explains the restaurant's menu to newcomers. Bāo • logy's menu focuses on Taiwanese street food, including potstickers (pan-seared dumplings), gwa baos (Taiwanese sliders), and ruen bings (Taiwanese wraps). The menu continues to evolve as guests become familiar with the offerings and seek a deeper journey into the cultural cuisine of Taiwan.

1829 John F. Kennedy Blvd., 215-999-2263

baology.com

DON'T MISS: Bao comes from a Chinese word with multiple meanings. It can mean bun, package, or bag or be the act of wrapping, filling, or packaging.

Highly coveted reservations

One of the hardest places in the city to get reservations is Laurel, Nicholas Elmi's intimate restaurant on East Passyunk. Its twenty-two seats are highly sought after by diners who want to try Elmi's delicately crafted, French-influenced cuisine. The restaurant offers a seven-course prix fixe menu with optional wine pairings. Although Laurel has a full bar, diners may bring their own bottle without a corkage fee. Shortly after it opened, Laurel was named to *GQ*'s list of most outstanding restaurants. In 2014, Elmi earned two James Beard semifinalist nominations, and he earned two more the following year.

The good news is that Elmi has since opened two more restaurants—ITV, a cocktail bar with well-executed snacks, next door to Laurel, and Old City's Royal Boucherie, a modern homage to classic French bistros with a charcuterie program and raw bar. These two cocktail-focused venues enable diners to enjoy Elmi's deft cuisine in more relaxed settings and offer creative beverage programs.

Some diners will recognize Elmi from winning season eleven of Bravo's *Top Chef*, but it was his years of training that made him a winner. After training with Guy Savoy Restaurant in Paris, Union Pacific, Oceana, and Lutèce in New York City, Elmi landed in Philadelphia, working at Le Bec Fin. The uber-formal French restaurant, which was opened nearly four decades earlier by Chef Georges Perrier, was internationally known. Many of the city's top chefs worked there, making it partially responsible for Philadelphia's restaurant renaissance. Elmi was the final chef at the restaurant before today's more relaxed dining habits contributed to its closure in 2013.

The final months before the closing of Perrier's Le Bec Fin were recorded in a documentary called *King Georges*. Perrier, a Frenchman with a well-earned reputation for being temperamental, was especially high-strung during those turbulent months. Throughout

Left: Chef Nicholas Elmi. Photo by Michael Spain-Smith.

Right: Arctic Char Crudo at ITV. Photo by Irene Levy Baker.

the ordeal, even when dishes were crashing and tongues were lashing, Elmi treated Perrier with reverence and respect. Near the end of the documentary there's a touching scene showing the two of them together again, but this time they're not in Perrier's former restaurant but instead at Elmi's new restaurant, Laurel.

Laurel
1617 E. Passyunk Ave., 215-271-8299
restaurantlaurel.com

ITV
1615 E. Passyunk Ave., 267-858-0669
itvphilly.com

Royal Boucherie
52 S. 2nd St., 267-606-6313
royalboucherie.com

DON'T MISS: Reservations for Laurel are available on Open Table two months ahead to the day. For reservations further out, call the restaurant directly. In warmer months, ask about Laurel's private chef's table in the backyard. It seats up to 8 people.

Bring Your Own Bottle

It can be difficult and costly for new restaurants to get a liquor license, thanks to Pennsylvania's Quaker background and its archaic liquor laws. Philadelphia restaurateurs have turned lemons into limoncello by opening BYOB—bring your own bottle—establishments. The trend has spawned many small, chef-driven restaurants, mom-and-pop shops, and ethnic eateries and energized the area's restaurant scene. Diners can bring their own wine, beer, or spirits, sidestepping the typical markup on liquor. BYOB allows wine connoisseurs to pair their good bottles with an equally good meal. Some BYOBs provide mixers, especially for Bloody Marys or mimosas, for brunch. A few hybrids, such as Laurel, serve alcohol but also let you bring your own or have BYOB nights. Most restaurants do not charge a corkage fee, but some are cash only.

The liquor laws in Pennsylvania are starting to loosen up for purchasing liquor. Tourists or diners without their own collections can visit state liquor stores for wine and spirits and beer distributors for beer. Plus, wine and beer are also available at select grocery stores. Beer lovers can also get six-packs at some gas stations and a few restaurants and bars.

Some BYOBs mentioned in the book include Amano, Audrey Claire, Dim Sum Garden, EAT Café, Frieda, Metropolitan Cafe, Miss Rachel's Pantry, Mr. Martino's, Penang (wine only), Pizza Brain, Portabellos of Kennett Square, Saté Kampar, Talula's Table, Vientiane, Will, and Zeppoli.

Some restaurants that serve liquor still allow you to bring your own bottle on certain nights of the week or during certain hours with little or no corkage fee including Laurel (see page 190), Brigantessa, Davio's Philadelphia, Fond, Le Virtu, and Southwark (see page 28).

Top left: Audrey Claire. Photo by Rachel Baker.

Top right: Poached salmon, asparagus, watercress, and properly scrambled farm fresh eggs at Talula's Table. Photo by Jaeson Han.

Above left: Interior of Miss Rachel's Pantry. Photo by Rodger Holst.

Above right: Portabello's of Kennett Square. Photo by Christina Neu, Chester County Conference & Visitors Bureau.

PRIVATE DINING ROOMS

Impress your guests

Trying to impress your colleagues? Planning a rehearsal dinner? Or birthday party? Here's a list of restaurants with private or semiprivate spaces for groups. Many restaurants are also available for full or partial buyouts.

Barbuzzo—The private second-floor space holds up to eighty-five guests. The space has an upright piano, private bathrooms, a bar, and a kitchen. When you choose the menu, include the restaurant's salted caramel Budino for dessert. Your guests will thank you. (See page 196.)

Di Bruno Bros.—The second floor of its Rittenhouse location holds special events for up to one hundred guests. Events at Di Bruno are BYOB. (See page 60.)

Feliz Restaurants—These Mexican restaurants have a variety of private and semiprivate spaces, including a cozy private dining room with a fireplace that seats sixteen at Cantina Feliz in Fort Washington and a private dining room for sixteen at Taqueria Feliz in Manayunk. (See page 64.)

Frieda—This charming space can accommodate small semiprivate events or be rented for private events for up to one hundred. It's BYOB. (See page 10.)

Hungry Pigeon—This comfortable all-day cafe with a bar that serves shareable small plates and family-style dishes has a farm table for fourteen in a warm, semiprivate room. Vegetarian and vegan friendly. (See page 68.)

Kensington Quarters—This industrial chic space has a private room on the second floor with a private bar. Meals for twenty guests are served family style. For a unique twist, use the demo kitchen for a private butchering class. (See page 74.)

Left: Cantina Feliz Private Dining Room. Photo by Jason Varney.

Right: Chef and Butcher dinner at Kensington Quarters. Photo by Jen Bragen.

McGillin's Olde Ale House—This historic tavern has a second-floor party room with space for ninety. Big screen TVs, a stage with a microphone, and thirty beers on tap are available. (See page 12.)

Miss Rachel's Pantry, a vegan mecca in South Philadelphia, has a farm table for twelve in a charming retro setting and room for up to twenty-five for a six-course vegan meal with organic beverages. It's BYOB. (See page 38.)

Harp & Crown—For a private event that feels clandestine, consider the subterranean bar and two-lane bowling alley in Schulson Collective's Harp and Crown. It holds up to 70 people.

Also consider: Nomad Pizza (nomadpizzaco.com), Royal Boucherie (see page 190), Osteria (see page 146), Fork (see page 70), Vetri (see page 146), Moshulu (see page 104), Zahav (see page 48), plus restaurant groups, such as High Street Hospitality Group, Garces Group, Starr Restaurants, and CookNSolo Restaurants.

WE HEART 13TH STREET RESTAURANT GROUP

From seedy to spectacular

Concierges used to caution guests against walking down 13th Street, which was home to check-cashing joints and adult bookstores. Now, tourists and locals flock to the street to patronize its trendy restaurants and boutiques. That's thanks, in part, to Valerie Safran and Marcie Turney, who started opening restaurants and boutiques there under the name We Heart 13th Street. The serial entrepreneurs have been instrumental in helping transform the neighborhood, which is now called Midtown Village.

Midtown Village overlaps with the Gayborhood, which was officially recognized by the city of Philadelphia in 2007 and marked with rainbow-topped street signs and crosswalks. The area prides itself on open-mindedness, diversity, and independently owned and operated businesses.

Turney is the versatile chef behind the covey of restaurants, and her business and life partner, Safran, is the business owner/manager. Together, they own Barbuzzo, a buzzy Mediterranean restaurant with wood-fired pizza and homemade pasta; Lolita, featuring modern Mexican fare; Little Nonna's, a homey Italian-American spot with a charming outside courtyard; Jamonera, a Spanish wine bar serving small plates; and Bud & Marilyn's, a kitschy retro restaurant serving American classics.

DON'T MISS: Barbuzzo's budino, a salted caramel pudding with a dark chocolate crust, topped with vanilla bean caramel and sea salt and served in a half mason jar.

Top left: Jamonera. Photo by Jason Varney.

Top right: Valerie Safran and Chef Marcie Turney. Photo by Jason Varney.

Above left: Barbuzzo's Budino. Photo by Jason Varney.

Above right: Little Nonna's covered courtyard. Photo by Jason Varney.

The duo also own several shops on 13th Street, including Grocery Market & Catering, which sells gourmet groceries and prepared foods; Open House, with Philadelphia-centric gadgets and gifts; and Verde, offering jewelry, clothing and a selection of Marcie Blaine Artisanal Chocolates.

Barbuzzo, 110 S. 13th St., 215-546-9300, barbuzzo.com

Bud & Marilyn's, 1234 Locust St., 215-546-2220, budandmarilyns.com

Jamonera, 105 S. 13th St., 215-922-6061, jamonerarestaurant.com

Little Nonna's, 1234 Locust St., 215-546-2100, littlenonnas.com

Lolita, 106 S. 13th St., 215-546-7100, lolitaphilly.com

A Renaissance man

Chef Jose Garces is more than a serial restaurateur. He's also an author, farmer, and philanthropist. He came to Philadelphia in 2001 to work for Stephen Starr (see page 200) and opened his first restaurant, Amada, in Philadelphia just four years later. In the years since, Garces has become a dominant force in Philadelphia's restaurant scene and has opened more restaurants in New York; Washington, D.C.; and Atlantic City. Garces won a James Beard Foundation Award for Best Chef, Mid-Atlantic in 2009 and is a Food Network Iron Chef.

Garces, who was born in Ecuador and raised in Chicago, specializes in Latin American/Spanish cuisine with a modern flare, but he doesn't limit himself to the genre he learned from his paternal grandmother. His restaurants range from a neighborhood pizzeria to Spanish tapas, and he has trained staff that have spun off to create their own beloved restaurants.

He's the author of two books, *The Latin Road Home* and *Latin Evolution*, and owns a forty-acre organic farm in Bucks County, called Luna.

Garces gives back to the community through the Garces Foundation, which is dedicated to Philadelphia's underserved immigrant communities, many of whom work in the restaurant industry. The foundation is focused on increasing access to health and educational services.

> **DON'T MISS:** The burger at Village Whiskey, a pub with a legendary whiskey list, or the Ecuadorian Shrimp Ceviche, a dish Chef Jose Garces has been eating his whole life and that he does riffs on in many of his restaurants.

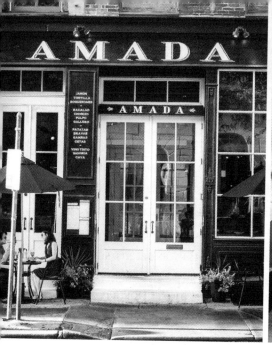

Left: Amada exterior. Photo by Steve Legato.

Right: Chef Jose Garces. Photo by Jason Varney.

Garces Restaurants in Philadelphia

garcesgroup.com

Amada—Spanish tapas in a high-energy setting
217-219 Chestnut St.

Buena Onda—Fast-casual tacos and margaritas
1901 Callowhill St.

Distrito—Mexican cuisine and full bar in vibrant setting
3945 Chestnut St.

JG Domestic—Farm-fresh ingredients convenient to 30th St. Station
2929 Arch St.

The Olde Bar—Seafood and cocktails in former home of Bookbinders (see page 162)
125 Walnut St.

Tinto—Basque Tapas in casual, elegant setting
114 S. 20th St.

Village Whiskey—Known for burger and whiskey selection
118 S. 20th St.

Volvér—Upscale restaurant in the Kimmel Center for the Performing Arts
300 S. Broad St.

A stellar lineup of restaurants

When Stephen Starr was a little boy, he wanted to be a radio deejay or a movie producer. Perhaps it's that desire to entertain that has made him so successful. Sure, the ability to spot a trend, pick a great location, find talented chefs, and maybe a little luck all helped as well. But it is his desire to entertain and his attention to details, such as music and lighting, that gives his restaurants energy and makes them shine.

After selling his concert promotion business in 1993, Starr struggled to figure out what he would produce next. He took a gamble that his understanding of how to sell concert tickets would translate into the ability to promote a restaurant. He saw the martini trend coming and felt that he could create the type of place where he'd like to hang out and, hopefully, that other people would too. They did! In fact, they lined up around the block to get into his martini bar called Continental.

Starr filled his constellation with great food, new concepts, and over-the-top decor. Each restaurant, such as Parc Restaurant, Bistro and Cafe, Morimoto, Talula's Garden, and Buddakan, has a distinct personality that carries through in its cuisine and atmosphere, from Cuban to Japanese and from a pizzeria to an enchanted garden. He believes that Philadelphia, where he had to rely on repeat customers rather than transient business, was the perfect place to hone his skills before taking his show on the road, opening restaurants in Atlantic City; Miami; Fort Lauderdale; Washington, D.C.; Paris; and then New York City. While he's yet to produce a movie, he did win what is considered the Oscar of the food industry, a coveted James Beard Award for Outstanding Restaurateur in 2017.

Left: Buddakan. Photo by Marissa Evans.

Right: Morimoto. Photo by Max Grudzinski.

Starr Restaurants in Philadelphia

starr-restaurants.com

Alma de Cuba—modern Latin cuisine
1623 Walnut St.

Barclay Prime—luxury boutique
steakhouse
237 S. 18th St.

Buddakan—modern Asian cuisine
325 Chestnut St.

Butcher and Singer—steaks and chops
in old Hollywood style
1500 Walnut St.

**Continental & Continental
Mid-Town**—restaurant and martini bar
1801 Chestnut St.
138 Market St.

The Dandelion—English pub
130 S. 18th St.

El Rey—Mexican (see page 83)
2013 Chestnut St.

El Vez—Mexican-American
121 S.13th St.

Fette Sau—smoked meat and craft beer
(see page 74)
1208 Frankford Ave.

Frankford Hall—beer garden
1210 Frankford Ave.

Jones—American comfort food
700 Chestnut St.

The Love—a neighborhood bistro with
outside dining
130 S. 18th St.

Morimoto—Japanese by Iron Chef
Mashaharu Morimoto
723 Chestnut St.

Parc Restaurant, Bistro and Cafe—
French bistro with outside dining across
from Rittenhouse Square
227 S. 18th St.

Pizzeria Stella—pizzeria
420 S. 2nd St.

Pod—contemporary Pan Asian
3636 Sansom St.

Serpico—global fare by James Beard-
award winning Chef Peter Serpico
604 South St.

Talula's Daily—casual sibling of
Talula's Garden
208 W. Washington Square

Talula's Garden—seasonal American
food inspired by the farm and garden
210 W. Washington Square

RESTAURANTS A-Z

a.kitchen+a.bar
135 S. 18th St.

A Mano
2244 Fairmount Ave.

Abe Fisher
1623 Sansom St.

Alma de Cuba
1623 Walnut St.

Amada
217-219 Chestnut St.

Ambra
705 S. 4th St.

Amis Trattoria
412 S. 13th St.

Audrey Claire
276 S. 20th St.

Aurora Grace Chocolates
auroragracechocolates.com

b.good
26 Centerton Rd.
Mount Laurel, NJ

150 Main St.
King of Prussia, PA

500 Rte 73 South
Marlton, NJ

bāo • logy
1829 John F. Kennedy Blvd.

Bar Amis
4503 S. Broad St.

Bar Bombón
133 S. 18th St.

Barbuzzo
110 S. 13th St.

Barclay Prime
237 S. 18th St.

Bassetts Ice Cream
Reading Terminal Market
51 N. 12th St.

Beiler's Doughnuts
Reading Terminal Market
51 N. 12th St.

3900 Chestnut St.

Bing Bing Dim Sum
1648 E. Passyunk Ave.

Bistro Romano
120 Lombard St.

Black Powder Tavern
1164 Valley Forge Rd.
Wayne, PA

Blue Sage Vegetarian Grille
727 2nd St. Pike
Southampton, PA

Bok Bar
800 Mifflin St.

Brigantessa
1520 E. Passyunk Ave.

Bud & Marilyn's
1234 Locust St.

Buddakan
325 Chestnut St.

Buena Onda
1901 Callowhill St.

Butcher and Singer
1500 Walnut St.

Cantina Feliz
424 S. Bethlehem Pike
Fort Washington, PA

Capofritto Pizzeria & Gelateria
233 Chestnut St.

Capogiro Gelato Artisans
119 S. 13th St.

117 S. 20th St.

1625 E. Passyunk Ave.

Center City Soft Pretzel
816 Washington Ave.

Charlie was a sinner
131 S. 13th St.

Cheu Fishtown
1416 Frankford Ave.

Cheu Noodle
255 S. 10th St.

Chinatown Square
1016-1018 Race St.

Citizens Bank Park
One Citizens Bank Way

City Tavern
138 S. 2nd St.

Continental
138 Market St.

Continental Midtown
1801 Chestnut St.

COOK
253 S. 20th St.

Crêperie Beau Monde
624 S. 6th St.

Culinary Literacy Center
Free Library of Philadelphia
1901 Vine St., 4th floor

The Dandelion
130 S. 18th St.

Dante & Luigi's
762 S. 10th St.

Day By Day
2101 Sansom St.

Di Bruno Bros.
930 S. 9th St.

1730 Chestnut St.

Comcast Center
1701 JFK Blvd.

834 Chestnut St.

120 Coulter Ave., Ardmore, PA

Dim Sum Garden
1020 Race St.

Distrito
3945 Chestnut St.

Dizengoff
1625 Sansom St.

EAT Café
3820 Lancaster Ave.

Éclat Chocolate
24 S. High St., West Chester, PA

El Compadre
1149 S. 9th St.

El Rey
2013 Chestnut St.

El Vez
121 S. 13th St.

Evil Genius
1727 Front St.

Fante's Kitchen Shop
1006 S. 9th St.

Farmer's Keep
10 S. 20th St.

Federal Distilling
1700 N. Hancock St.

Federal Donuts
1219 S. 2nd St.

1632 Sansom St.

3428 Sansom St.

701 N. 7th St.

Whole Foods
2101 Pennsylvania Ave.

Citizens Bank Park
One Citizens Bank Way

Ferry Market
32 S. Main St., New Hope, PA

Fette Sau
1208 Frankford Ave.

Fitzwater Station
264 Canal St., Phoenixville, PA

Five Saints Distilling
129 E. Main St., Norristown, PA

Fork
306 Market St.

Frankford Hall
1210 Frankford Ave.

The Franklin Fountain
116 Market St.

Franklin Ice Cream Bar
112 Market St.

Franklin Mortgage and Investment Company
112 S. 18th St.

Frieda
320 Walnut St.

Front Street Cafe
1253 N. Front St.

Fu-Wah Mini Market
810 S. 47th St.

General Warren
9 Old Lancaster Rd., Malvern, PA

Geno's Steaks
1219 S. 9th St.

Goldie
1526 Sansom St.

Good Soup
1400 N. Front St.

Gran Caffè L'Aquila
1716 Chestnut St.

Green Eggs Cafe
1306 Dickinson St.

719 N. 2nd St.

212 S. 13th St.

Green Soul
1410 Mt. Vernon St.

Greensgrow Farms
2501 E. Cumberland St.

The Grille Room in the Mask and Wig Club
310 S. Quince St.

The Happy Mixer
4275 County Line Rd. Chalfont, PA

Ferry Market
32 S. Main St., New Hope, PA

12 Summit Sq., Langhorne, PA

Harp & Crown
1525 Sansom St.

Hearthside
801 Haddon Ave.
Collingswood, NJ

Herschel's East Side Deli
Reading Terminal Market
51 N. 12th St.

High Street Market
308 Market St.

Hip City Vedge
127 S. 18th St.

121 S. Broad St.

214 S. 40th St.

301 S. Christopher Columbus Blvd.

Honey's Sit N Eat
2101 South St.

800 N. 4th St.

Hop Sing Laundromat
1029 Race St.

Hungry Pigeon
743 S. 4th St.

Independence Beer Garden
100 S. Independence Mall West

ITV
1615 E. Passyunk Ave.

JG Domestic
2929 Arch St.

Jamonera
105 S. 13th St.

Japanese Tea Ceremony
Horticultural and Lansdowne Drives, West Fairmount Park

John & Kira's
johnandkiras.com

John's Water Ice
701 Christian St.

7315 Park Ave., Pennsauken, NJ

Jones
700 Chestnut St.

Kaplan's New Model Bakery
901 N. Third St.

Kensington Quarters
1310 Frankford Ave.

Kimmel Center for the
Performing Arts
300 S. Broad St.

La Calaca Feliz
2321 Fairmount Ave.

La Colombe
130 S. 19th St.

1335 Frankford Ave.

1414 S. Penn Square

100 S. Independence Mall West

La Michoacana
231 E. State St.
Kennett Square, PA

La Veranda
Penn's Landing, Pier 3

Laurel
1617 E. Passyunk Ave.

Little Baby's Ice Cream
2311 Frankford Ave.

4903 Catharine St.

Little Nonna's
1234 Locust St.

Lolita
106 S. 13th St.

London Grill
2301-2302 Fairmount Ave.

The Love
130 S. 18th St.

Mac Mart
104 S. 18th St.

Magpie
1622 South St.

Maison 208
208 S.13th St.

Mama's Vegetarian
18 S. 20th St.

McGillin's Olde Ale House
1310 Drury St.

Metropolitan Bakery
262 S. 19th St.

4013 Walnut St.

Reading Terminal Market
51 N. 12th St.

Metropolitan Cafe & Pizza
264 S. 19th St.

Miller's Twist
Reading Terminal Market
51 N. 12th St.

Miss Rachel's Pantry
1938 S. Chadwick St.

Morimoto
723 Chestnut St.

Moshulu
401 S. Columbus Blvd.

Mountain Laurel Spirits
925 Canal St., Bristol, PA

Mr. Martino's Trattoria
1646 E. Passyunk Ave.

Mueller Chocolate Co.
Reading Terminal Market
51 N. 12th St.

The Mushroom Cap
114 W. State St.
Kennett Square, PA

Nuts To You
22-24 S. 20th St.

1328 Walnut St.

1500 Market St.

721 Walnut St.

10861 Bustleton Ave.

The Olde Bar
125 Walnut St.

Oloroso
1121 Walnut St.

One Tippling Place
2006 Chestnut St.

Osteria
640 N. Broad St.

Oyster House
1516 Sansom St.

P. S. & Co.
1706 Locust St.

Palizzi Social Club
1408 S.12th St.

**Parc Restaurant, Bistro
and Cafe**
227 S. 18th St.

Pat's King of Steaks
1237 E. Passyunk Ave.

Penang
117 N. 10th St.

Philadelphia Brewing Company
2440 Frankford Ave.

Philadelphia Distilling
25 E. Allen St.

Pizza Brain
2313 Frankford Ave.

Pizzeria Stella
420 S. 2nd St.

Pizzeria Vetri
1939 Callowhill St.

1615 Chancellor St.

640 W. DeKalb Pike
King of Prussia, PA

Pod
3636 Sansom St.

Pop's Homemade Italian Ice
1337 Oregon Ave.

150 W. Eagle Rd.
Havertown, PA

Portabellos of Kennett Square
108 E. State St.
Kennett Square, PA

Posh Pop Bakeshop
109 Kings Highway East
Haddonfield, NJ

Ralph's Italian Restaurant
760 S. 9th St.

Rangoon
112 N. 9th St.

Ranstead Room
2013 Ranstead St.

Ray's Café & Tea House
141 N. 9th St.

Reading Terminal Market
51 N.12th St.

Relish
7152 Ogontz Ave.

RIM Café
1172 S. 9th St.

Rita's Water Ice
Throughout the country

Rival Bros. Coffee Roasters
2400 Lombard St.

1528 Spruce St.

1100 Tasker St.

Rooster Soup Company
1526 Sansom St.

Rosa's Fresh Pizza
25 S. 11th St.

16 S. 40th St.

Rowhouse Spirits
2440 Frankford Ave.

Royal Boucherie
52 S. 2nd St.

Sabrina's Café
901 Christian St.

1804 Callowhill St.

227 N. 34th St.

50 E. Wynnewood Rd.
Wynnewood, PA

714 Haddon Ave.
Collingswood, NJ

Saté Kampar
1837 E. Passyunk Ave.

Savona
100 Old Gulph Rd.
Gulph Mills, PA

Sciascia Confections
Ferry Market
32 S. Main St.
Yardley, PA

Stockton Market
19 Bridge St.
Stockton, NJ

Serpico
604 South St.

Shane Confectionery
110 Market St.

Skyline Terrace
Free Library of Philadelphia
1901 Vine St.

South
600 N. Broad St.

Southwark
701 S. 4th St.

Sprig & Vine
450 Union Square Drive
New Hope, PA

Spruce Street Harbor Park
Columbus Blvd. at Spruce St.

Suraya
1528 Frankford Ave.

Sweet Freedom
1424 South St.

1039 W. Lancaster Ave.
Bryn Mawr, PA

Taffets Bakery & Store
1024 S. 9th St.

Talula's Daily
208 W. Washington Square

Talula's Garden
210 W. Washington Square

Talula's Table
102 W. State St.
Kennett Square, PA

Taqueria Feliz
4410 Main St., Manayunk, PA

Tavern on Camac
243 S. Camac St.

Termini Bros. Bakery
1523 S. 8th St.

1538 Packer Ave.

Reading Terminal Market
51 N. 12th St.

Comcast Center
1701 JFK Blvd.

Tinto
114 S. 20th St.

Tired Hands Brew Café
16 Ardmore Ave., Ardmore, PA

Tired Hands Fermentaria
35 Cricket Terrace, Ardmore, PA

Tired Hands General Store
20 Ardmore Ave., Ardmore, PA

Townsend
1623 E. Passyunk Ave.

V Street
126 S. 19th St.

Vedge
1221 Locust St.

Vernick Food & Drink
2031 Walnut St.

Vetri Cucina
1312 Spruce St.

Victor Cafe
1303 Dickinson St.

Vientiane Café
4728 Baltimore Ave.

Vietnam Café
816 S. 47th St.

Vietnam Restaurant
221 N. 11th St.

Village Whiskey
118 S. 20th St.

Volvér
300 S. Broad St.

Warmdaddy's
1400 S. Columbus Blvd.

Wawa
Throughout the region

White Horse Tavern
707 E. Lancaster Ave.
Frazer, PA

Will BYOB
1911 E. Passyunk Ave.

Wiz Kid
124 S. 19th St.

The Woodlands at Phillips
1020 Kaolin Rd.
Kennett Square, PA

Wm. Mulherin's Sons
1355 N. Front St.

The Woodlands at Phillips
1020 Kaolin Rd.
Kennett Square, PA

Wynnewood Square Shopping Center
280 E. Lancaster Ave.
Wynnewood, PA

Yards Brewing
500 Spring Garden St.

Zahav
237 St. James Place

Zeppoli
618 W. Collings Ave.
Collingswood, NJ

APPENDIX

AVENUE OF THE ARTS
Hip City Veg, 21
Kimmel Center for the Performing Arts, 182
Volvér, 199

BENJAMIN FRANKLIN PARKWAY
Culinary Literacy Center, 110
Skyline Terrace, 182

CHINATOWN
Chinatown Square, 90
Dim Sum Garden, 90
Hop Sing Laundromat, 26
Penang, 90
Rangoon, 90
Ray's Café & Tea House, 90
Vietnam Restaurant, 40
Wok'N Walk Tours of Chinatown, 176

CONVENTION CENTER DISTRICT/ READING TERMINAL MARKET
Bassetts Ice Cream, 24
Beiler's Doughnuts, 144
Hershel's East Side Deli, 46
Metropolitan Bakery, 76
Miller's Twist, 144
Mueller Chocolate Co., 2
Reading Terminal Market, 148
Taste of Philly Food Tour, 148

FAIRMOUNT/FAIRMOUNT PARK
A Mano, 186
Buena Onda, 199
Federal Donuts, 50
Japanese Tea Ceremony, 102
La Calaca Feliz, 64

London Grill, 84
Pizzeria Vetri, 146
Sabrina's Café, 96

FISHTOWN/KENSINGTON
Cheu Fishtown, 78
Evil Genius, 74
Federal Distilling, 158
Fette Sau, 201
Frankford Hall, 201
Front Street Cafe, 20
Good Spoon, 74
Greensgrow Farms, 14
Kensington Quarters, 74
La Colombe, 142
Little Baby's Ice Cream, 94
Philadelphia Brewing Company, 154
Philadelphia Distilling, 158
Pizza Brain, 94
Rowhouse Spirits, 74
Suraya, 58
Wm Mulherin's Sons, 164

MANAYUNK
Taqueria Feliz, 64

MARKET STREET WEST
bāo • logy, 188
Di Bruno Bros., 60
Farmer's Keep, 136
La Colombe, 142
Mama's Vegetarian, 21
Nuts To You, 100
Termini Bros. Bakery, 80

MIDTOWN VILLAGE

Barbuzzo Mediterranean Kitchen and Bar, 196
Bud & Marilyn's, 196
Capogiro Gelato Artisans, 134
Charlie was a sinner, 20
Double Knot, 150
El Vez, 201
Green Eggs Cafe, 96
The Grille Room, 82
Jamonera, 196
Little Nonna's, 196
Lolita, 196
Maison 208, 114
McGillin's Olde Ale House, 12
Nuts To You, 100
Rosa's Fresh Pizza, 52
Tavern on Camac, 16

NORTH/NORTHEAST PHILLY/WEST OAK LANE

Federal Donuts, 50
Green Soul, 88
Nuts To You, 100
Osteria, 146
Relish, 88
South, 88

NORTHERN LIBERTIES

Green Eggs Cafe, 96
Honey's Sit N Eat, 97
Kaplan's New Model Bakery, 112
Yards Brewing, 154

OLD CITY/HISTORIC DISTRICT

Amada, 199
Capofritto Pizzeria & Gelateria, 134
City Tavern, 92
Continental, 201
Fork, 70
The Franklin Fountain, 106
Franklin Ice Cream Bar, 108
Frieda, 10

High Street on Market, 70
Independence Beer Garden, 182
Jones, 201
La Colombe, 142
Morimoto, 201
The Olde Bar, 162
Royal Boucherie, 190
Shane Confectionery, 108

RITTENHOUSE SQUARE/FITLER SQUARE

1 Tippling Place, 82
a.kitchen+bar, 70
Abe Fisher, 48
Alma de Cuba, 201
Audrey Claire, 192
Bar Bombón, 20
Barclay Prime, 201
Butcher and Singer, 201
Capogiro Gelato Artisans, 134
Continental Mid-Town, 201
COOK, 62
The Dandelion, 201
Davio's Philadelphia, 192
Day by Day, 96
Di Bruno Bros., 60
Dizengoff, 48
El Rey, 201
Federal Donuts, 50
Franklin Mortgage & Investment Company, 82
Goldie, 48
Gran Caffè L'Aquila, 8
Harp & Crown, 195
Hip City Veg, 21
La Colombe, 142
The Love, 201
Mac Mart, 174
Metropolitan Bakery/Cafe, 76
Nuts To You, 100
Oyster House, 66
P.S. & Co., 21

Metropolitan Bakery, 76
Pod, 201
Sabrina's Café, 96
Vientiane Café, 32
Vietnam Café, 40

WASHINGTON SQUARE/ WASHINGTON SQUARE WEST
Amis Trattoria, 146
Cheu Noodle Bar, 78
Di Bruno Bros., 60
Nuts To You, 100
Oloroso, 186
Talula's Daily, 201
Talula's Garden, 201
Vedge, 18
Vetri Cucina, 146

BUCKS COUNTY
Blue Sage Vegetarian Grille, 20
Ferry Market, 178
The Happy Mixer, 138
Mountain Laurel Spirits, 158
Sciascia Confections, 178
Sprig & Vine, 21

CHESTER COUNTY
Éclat Chocolate, 2
Fitzwater Station, 16
General Warren, 170
La Michoacana, 168
The Mushroom Cap, 168
Portabellos of Kennett Square, 34
Talula's Table, 86
White Horse Tavern, 170
The Woodlands at Phillips, 168

DELAWARE COUNTY
Black Powder Tavern, 170
Pop's Homemade Italian Ice, 36

MONTGOMERY COUNTY
b.good, 160
Cantina Feliz, 64
Di Bruno Bros., 60
Five Saints Distilling, 158
Pizzeria Vetri, 146
Sabrina's Cafe, 96
Savona, 170
Sweet Freedom Bakery, 136
Tired Hands, 154

SOUTH JERSEY
b.good, 160
Hearthside, 150
John's Water Ice, 36
Nomad Pizza, 195
Posh Pop Bakeshop, 138
Sabrina's Cafe, 96
Sciascia Confections, 178
Zeppoli, 22

THROUGHOUT PHILADELPHIA
Aurora Grace Chocolates, 2
John & Kira's, 2
Parks on Tap, 182
Restaurant Week, 180
Rita's Water Ice, 36
Wawa, 184

Parc Restaurant, Bistro, and Cafe, 200
Pizzeria Vetri, 146
Ranstead Room, 82
Rival Bros. Coffee Roasters, 166
Rooster Soup Company, 50
Tinto, 199
V Street, 18
Vernick Food & Drink, 72
Village Whiskey, 199
Wiz Kid, 18

SOCIETY HILL/DELAWARE WATERFRONT
Bistro Romano, 16
La Veranda, 7
Moshulu, 104
Spruce Street Harbor Park, 182
Warmdaddy's, 88
Zahav, 48

SOUTH PHILLY
9th Street Italian Market, 98
Bar Amis, 146
Barcelona Wine Bar, 98
Bing Bing Dim Sum, 78
Bok Bar, 182
Brigantessa, 98
Capogiro Gelato Artisans, 134
Center City Soft Pretzel, 144
Citizens Bank Park, 20
Dante & Luigi's Corona di Ferro, 6
Di Bruno Bros., 60
El Compadre, 54
Fante's Kitchen Shop, 172
Federal Donuts, 50
Fond, 98
Geno's Steaks, 156
Green Eggs Cafe, 96
ITV, 190
Italian Market Immersion, 98
John's Water Ice, 36
Laurel, 190

Le Virtu, 192
Miss Rachel's Pantry, 38
Mr. Martino's Trattoria, 30
Noord, 98
Palizzi Social Club, 22
Pat's King of Steaks, 156
Pop's Homemade Italian Ice, 36
Ralph's Italian Restaurant, 152
RIM Café, 56
Rival Bros. Coffee Roasters, 166
Sabrina's Cafe, 96
Saté Kampar, 44
Taffets Bakery, 139
Taste4Travel Tour, 98
Termini Bros. Bakery, 80
Townsend, 186
Victor Cafe, 140
Will BYOB, 4

SOUTH STREET/GRADUATE HOSPITAL/BELLA VISTA/QUEEN VILLAGE
Ambra, 28
Crêperie Beau Monde, 96
Honey's Sit N Eat, 97
Hungry Pigeon, 68
Magpie, 42
Nomad Pizza, 195
Pizzeria Stella, 201
Serpico, 201
Southwark, 28
Sweet Freedom Bakery, 136

UNIVERSITY CITY/WEST PHILLY
Beiler's Doughnuts, 144
Distrito, 199
EAT Café, 52
Federal Donuts, 50
Fu-Wah Mini Market, 40
Hip City Veg, 21
JG Domestic, 199
Little Baby's Ice Cream, 94